The First Book of
CorelDRAW!™ 3

Ray Werner

alpha
books

A Division of Prentice Hall Computer Publishing
11711 North College, Carmel, Indiana 46032 USA

To my daughter, Rita.

© **1992 by Alpha Books**

All rights reserved. No part of this book shall be reproduced, stored in a retrieval system, or transmitted by any means, electronic, mechanical, photocopying, recording, or otherwise, without written permission from the publisher. No patent liability is assumed with respect to the use of the information contained herein. Although every precaution has been taken in the preparation of this book, the publisher and author assume no responsibility for errors or omissions. Neither is any liability assumed for damages resulting from the use of the information contained herein. For information, address Alpha Books, 11711 N. College Ave., Carmel, IN 46032.

International Standard Book Number: 1-56761-007-2
Library of Congress Catalog Card Number: 92-72900

95 94 93 92   8 7 6 5 4 3 2 1

Interpretation of the printing code: the rightmost number of the first series of numbers is the year of the book's printing; the rightmost number of the second series of numbers is the number of the book's printing. For example, a printing code of 92-1 shows that the first printing of the book occurred in 1992.

Screen reproductions in this book were created by means of the program Collage Plus from Inner Media, Inc., Hollis, NH.

Printed in the United States of America

Publisher
Marie Butler-Knight

Managing Editor
Elizabeth Keaffaber

Product Development Manager
Lisa A. Bucki

Acquisitions Editor
Susan Orr Klopfer

Development Editor
Faithe Wempen

Production Editor
Lisa C. Hoffman

Copy Editor
Audra Gable

Cover Design
Jay Corpus

Cover Illustration
Polly McNeal

Indexer
Loren Malloy

Production Team
Christine Cook,
Lisa Daugherty,
Terri Edwards,
Mark Enochs,
Tim Groeling,
Joelynn Gifford,
Dennis Clay Hager,
John Kane,
Carrie Keesling,
Phil Kitchel,
Bob LaRoche,
Thomas Loveman,
Matthew Morrill,
Michael J. Nolan,
Linda Quigley,
Michelle Self,
Susan Shepard,
Angie Trzepacz,
Mary Beth Wakefield,
Julie Walker,
Kelli Widdifield

Special thanks to C. Herbert Feltner
for assuring the technical accuracy of this book.

Contents

1 Getting Started with CorelDRAW! 3 **3**

Starting CorelDRAW! 4
The CorelDRAW! Desktop 6
    The Menu Bar 7
    The File Menu 10
    New 10
    Open… 10
    Save As… 10
    Import… 10
    Export… 11
    Object… 11
    Print… 11
    Print Merge… 11
    Print Setup… 11
    Page Setup 11
    Exit 12
    1,2,3,4 12
Quitting CorelDRAW! 12

2 Putting CorelDRAW! to Work **15**

Drawing Objects 19
    Drawing Lines..20
Drawing Rectangles, Squares,
  Ellipses, and Circles 21
Selecting, Moving, Scaling, and Sizing Objects 22
What's Next?—Skewing and Rotating Objects 24

3 Zooms, Rulers, and Grids **29**

Using Rulers 29
    Changing the Zero Points of the Rulers 31
Zooming the Display 32
Drawing Using a Grid 35
Project 1— Geometric Art 36
What's Next?—Using Wireframe View 37

4 Saving and Printing   41

Saving a File 41
Getting Ready to Print 43
    Changing Print Options 44
Printing a Drawing 45
What's Next?—Keywords and Notes 47

5 Jazzing Up the Line   51

Reopening the Drawing 51
The Outline Pen 52
    Opening the Pen Roll-Up Window 53
    More Line Thickness Control 54
    Adding Arrows to Lines 54
Dotted or Dashed Lines 56
Changing Outline Color 57
    Advanced Color Selection 58
Using Your New Skills 59
Grouping Objects 60
    Grouping Selected Objects 61
Scaling, Duplicating, and Mirroring 62
    Scaling 62
    Duplicating 63
What's Next?—More on Object Alignment 66
    Guidelines 66
    Nudging 67

6 Drawing Curves, Circles, and Segments   71

Curving a Straight Line 71
    Drawing Freehand 72
    Drawing in Bézier Mode 73
    Using the Shape Tool 75
    Shaping Lines and Curves 77

7 Nodes and Fills   81

What Is a Node? 81
Opening the Node Edit Dialog Box 82
Changing the Type of Node 83
   Smooth Node 83
   Symmetrical Node 84
   Cusp Node 85
Adding and Deleting Nodes 86
Project 2—Making a Cloud 87
Using Fills 88
What's Next?—Combining Tools and Objects 93

8 Adding and Editing Text   97

About Fonts 97
Adding Text 98
   Adding Artistic Text 99
   Adding Paragraph Text 100
   Adding Text with the Clipboard 101
   Importing Text 103
Editing and Formatting Text 104
   Using the Text Roll-Up Window 106
Changing the Paragraph Text Frame 107
Adding Symbols 109
What's Next?—Using the Spelling Checker
and Thesaurus 111

9 Advanced Text Manipulation   115

Adjusting Text Spacing 115
   Advanced Spacing Options 117
Copying Text Attributes 118
Fitting Text to a Path 119
   Creating The Apple Corps Logo 120
   Controlling How Letters Sit on a Path 123
   Designating the Distance from the Path 125
   Adjusting Path Alignment 126

10 Special Effects, Part I   **131**

Perspective 131
   Adding Perspective 132
   Altering Perspective 134
   Multiple-Point Perspective 135
   Copying Perspective 136
Shaping with Envelopes 138
   What's Next?—Copying an Envelope 142

11 Special Effects, Part II   **145**

Changing Perspective and Depth 148
Rotating a Perspective Extrusion 150
Creating Shading Effects 151
Coloring the Extrusion 152
Seeing How It All Works Together 153
What's Next?—Blending 156
   Blending Objects Along a Path 158

12 A Color Primer   **163**

Conventional Separation Process 164
   Color Separations in CorelDRAW! 165
Process Colors 165
   The CMYK Model 165
   The RGB Model 167
   The HSB Model 168
   The Palette Model 169
   The Names Model 169
Spot Colors 170
   PostScript Options 171
Summary 173

**A Using DISKCOPY
to Make Backup Disks**   **175**

B Microsoft Windows Primer   **177**

   Starting Windows 178
   The Windows Interface 178

Using a Mouse 179
Using the Keyboard 180
Managing Directories and Files............................181
Making Directories with the File Manager 182
Selecting Files To Copy, Move, or Delete 182
Copying Files 183
Moving Files..183
Deleting Files 184
For More Information 184

C Installing CorelDRAW!   185

System Requirements 185
Installing CorelDRAW! 186

D Customizing CorelDRAW!   191

Setting General Preferences 191
Place Duplicate 192
Nudge 192
Constrain Angle 192
Miter Limit..192
Auto-Panning 193
Cross Hair Cursor 193
Interruptible Display 193
Setting Curve Preferences 193
Freehand Tracking 194
Autotrace Tracking 194
Corner Threshold 194
Straight Line Threshold 194
AutoJoin 195
Setting Display Preferences 195
Preview Fountain Stripes 195
Greek Text Below 196
Preview Colors 196
Curve Flatness 196
Customizing the Secondary Mouse Button 197

Index   199

Introduction

Welcome to CorelDRAW! 3. If you have already purchased the program, congratulations. If you are reading this book to see if CorelDRAW! 3 is for you, I am happy to be of assistance. You should know right up front, however, that I really like this program. I will try to keep my enthusiasm within proper bounds, but if I fall over the edge from time to time, try to understand.

CorelDRAW! has long had the reputation of being a top-of-the-line graphics package for the personal computer operating in the MS-DOS environment. Quite simply, release 3 of CorelDRAW! takes this reputation to a new height. It is easy to learn, very powerful, and a lot of fun to use.

This book will explore some of the program's many features, and by the time you finish, you'll be a competent CorelDRAW! craftsperson.

What Does CorelDRAW! Do That a Paint Program Won't?

Paint programs, like Microsoft Windows Paintbrush, are designed to work much the same way as an artist does—you apply color to a canvas. The canvas is the computer monitor, and color is applied by turning individual dots (pixels) on the screen on or off. The computer keeps track of a drawing made by a paint program by keeping a map of all of the pixels that make up the drawing. (This is why they are called bit-mapped graphics.)

It is difficult to modify the size of a bit-mapped image. If, for example, you wanted to double the size of a drawing, the program would accomplish this by making each pixel two pixels. The results can often appear like those in Figure I.1, as distorted images and lines with jagged edges.

Figure I.1

Bit-mapped graphics lose their attractiveness and can become distorted when their size is modified.

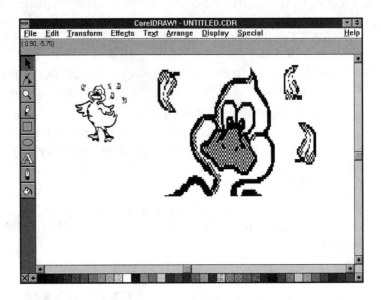

CorelDRAW! represents a completely different type of graphics program, commonly called a draw program. Instead of mapping each pixel, this program stores images as a series of equations. Modifying the size of an object in a draw program is a much simpler proposition (for you) and the results are much more pleasing.

For example, when you modify the size of a circle, the program will calculate its new diameter. The thickness of the lines is not changed, as it would be in a paint program. In a draw program, the quality of the image is not affected by a modification to the size (see Figure I.2).

In a draw program, the image is stored as one object rather than as individual pixels. Therefore, graphics composed in a draw program are often called vector art or object-oriented art.

Figure I.2
Vector graphics do not deteriorate in quality even when increased to many times their original size.

Where Does CorelDRAW! Fit within the Desktop Publishing World?

We have already learned that CorelDRAW! can develop art that can be expanded or reduced without affecting its quality. This is, of course, very important in areas such as advertising, publishing, and commercial art.

However, CorelDRAW! also gives the artist the capability to control colors, contrast, and perspective to a point that can rival a 35mm slide! This power makes CorelDRAW! a perfect tool to use with professional text development software such as Aldus PageMaker, Ventura Publisher, or QuarkXpress. It will often be found on the shelf in any PC-capable design studio.

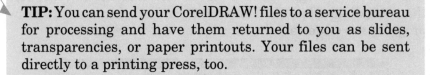

TIP: You can send your CorelDRAW! files to a service bureau for processing and have them returned to you as slides, transparencies, or paper printouts. Your files can be sent directly to a printing press, too.

However, you do not have to be a professional designer to use CorelDRAW! And, you do not need Aldus PageMaker, Ventura Publisher, or Quark Xpress to fully utilize the program's capabilities. CorelDRAW! is perfectly capable of producing text for a complete document, spell-checking it, designing or importing and placing clip art, and printing camera-ready copy. CorelDRAW! 3 even includes a thesaurus!

Get Ready to Draw!

The rest of this book will assume that you have CorelDRAW! installed on your system. If you are having problems installing it, please refer to Appendix A for instructions.

CorelDRAW! will work on any system that is capable of running Windows, but it works best in Enhanced mode. In addition, before you start CorelDRAW!, keep the following hints in mind:

- Corel Systems recommends that you use Windows 3.1.

- You can't have enough memory, but you will need at least 4M of RAM—eight is better. (I am running with 20M and have topped out a couple of times.)

- Graphics files take up a lot of room. Be sure that you have ample free space on your hard drive, more than 5M, before you try to manipulate any complex images.

- It is very difficult to get along without a mouse.

Conventions Used in This Book

As you use this book, you will notice that it includes several special elements to highlight important information.

- Actions that you take, whether it's pressing a key, selecting a menu, or typing a word, will appear in color.

- Text that you should type in is printed in a `bold, color computer font like this`.

- Keys that you press are shown as keycaps, like ⏎Enter and Tab↹. When keycaps are mentioned in passing, they will appear like this: ⏎Enter and Tab↹.

- Many commands are activated by pressing two or more keys at the same time. These key presses or selections are separated by a plus sign (+) in the text. For example, "press Alt+F1" means that you should hold down the Alt key while you press F1. (You don't type the plus sign.)

- Other commands are activated by selecting a menu and then an option. A command like "select File New" means that you should open the File menu and select the New option from it. In this book, the selection letter is printed in boldface for easy recognition.

QUICK STEPS

Look for this icon for Quick Steps that tell you how to perform important tasks in CorelDRAW!. Quick Steps and the page numbers on which they appear are listed on the inside front cover of this book.

TIP: Helpful tips and shortcuts are included in Tip boxes.

Practical ideas for using CorelDRAW! are outlined in these boxes.

NOTE: Important information that should be noted when using CorelDRAW! is included here.

These are potential pitfalls and problems which you should avoid when using CorelDRAW!.

Acknowledgments

I have several people to thank for seeing this project to its completion. First and foremost are my parents. Their help and encouragement through some difficult times were far above the call of duty. Thank you, I love you.

I don't know how Alpha did it, but they managed to gather together, and assign to me, some of the most competent and professional editors that I have ever dealt with, and I have dealt with a bunch.

Susan, my answering machine will accept your free-association calls anytime.

Faithe, gosh you're good, and the copy is in the courier's hands.

Lise (Lisa Hoffman), what a job!

And, lurking somewhere in the background, is Herb Feltner, my technical editor. This person's job is to keep my foot out of my mouth. You be the judge.

Trademarks

All terms mentioned in this book that are known to be trademarks or service marks are listed below. In addition, terms suspected of being trademarks or service marks have been appropriately capitalized. Alpha Books cannot attest to the accuracy of this information. Use of a term in this book should not be regarded as affecting the validity of any trademark or service mark.

Aldus PageMaker is a registered trademark of the Aldus Corporation.

Ccapture, CorelDRAW!, CorelMOSAIC!, Corel PHOTO-PAINT, and CorelTRACE! are trademarks of Corel Systems Corporation.

MS-DOS is a registered trademark of the Microsoft Corporation.

Windows is a trademark of the Microsoft Corporation.

QuarkXPress is a registered trademark of Quark, Inc.

Ventura Publisher is a registered trademark of Ventura Software, Inc.

In This Chapter

Starting CorelDRAW!

The CorelDRAW! Desktop

Opening a Pull-Down Menu

Creating a New File

Quitting CorelDRAW!

Starting CorelDRAW! from Windows

1. Open the CorelDRAW! program group window.
2. Double-click on the CorelDRAW! icon.

Opening a Menu

- Click on the menu name.
- Press [Alt] and the bold letter in the desired menu name.

Selecting a Command from an Open Menu

- Click on the desired command.
- Type the underlined selection letter in the command's name.

Creating a New File

1. Open the File menu.
2. Select New.

Quitting CorelDRAW!

1. Open the File menu.
2. Select Exit.

Getting Started with CorelDRAW! 3

I t is time to start learning about CorelDRAW!. In this chapter, we will start the program and begin to learn about the desktop.

If you're new to the Windows environment, take some time to become comfortable with Windows before attempting this chapter. Complete the tutorial that comes with Windows, and learn about the special terms that are used in Windows programs. Terms such as click, double-click, drag, and drop will be used throughout this book. See the section on Windows in the Introduction for some beginning-level help.

If you have not installed CorelDRAW! onto your hard disk yet (that is, if it doesn't appear in your Windows Program Manager as a program group or icon), see Appendix A now. This section will show you how to install CorelDRAW! for your system. You must have Windows 3.x (preferably 3.1) installed before you can install CorelDRAW!. The procedure for installing Windows is covered in the *Windows User's Guide*.

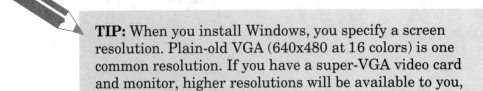

TIP: When you install Windows, you specify a screen resolution. Plain-old VGA (640x480 at 16 colors) is one common resolution. If you have a super-VGA video card and monitor, higher resolutions will be available to you, as well as a 256-color option.

Some people think it's important to use as high a screen resolution as possible when working with graphic images. Maybe for a professional designer this is true, but not for a beginner. Higher screen resolutions make for smaller images that are harder to focus on. I have found that the best learning resolution for me is 640x480 with 256 colors. If possible, try to duplicate this. (Use the Windows Setup program to change screen resolution.) Your eyes and temper will thank you for it later.

Starting CorelDRAW!

If Windows is not started on your system, type WIN at the DOS prompt and press ↵Enter. Then you can start CorelDRAW! as you would start any Windows application. The following Quick Steps show how.

Starting CorelDraw!

1. If it's not already open, open the Corel Graphics group window by double-clicking on its icon.

    Figure 1.1 shows an example of the open Corel Graphics application group.

2. Double-click on the CorelDRAW! icon.

    CorelDRAW! opens displaying a new, blank screen. Figure 1.2 shows the screen at this point.

NOTE: For most procedures in Windows, you can use either a mouse or the keyboard. However, having a mouse is virtually a necessity when using CorelDRAW! because the mouse helps you draw. The following Quick Steps, and many others in this book, assume that you have a mouse.

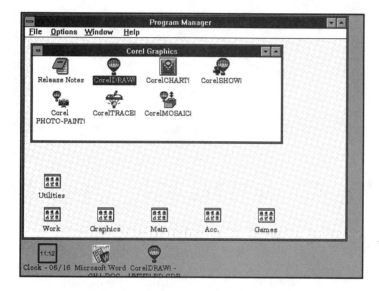

Figure 1.1
The CorelDRAW! group window.

TIP: Click on a window to bring it to the surface so you can view its contents.

Figure 1.2
The CorelDRAW!
workspace.

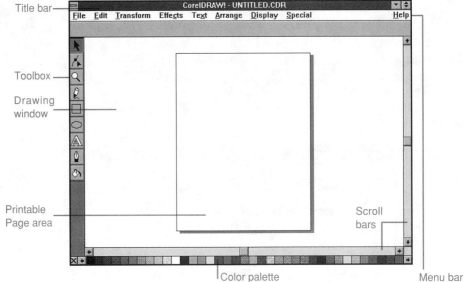

Title bar

Toolbox

Drawing
window

Printable
Page area

Scroll
bars

Color palette

Menu bar

The CorelDRAW! Desktop

Your screen may differ in some respects from Figure 1.2. (For example, a ruler may appear at the top of your screen, or the page outline might not be visible.) One of the major benefits of a program like CorelDRAW! is its ability to be modified to suit the users' needs or desires.

Here is a brief description of each component of the CorelDRAW! screen. Most of these are shown in Figure 1.2.

The **title bar** tells you the name of the program and the name of the drawing that is active.

The **menu bar** contains nine pull-down menus. These menus, and their uses, will be discussed in greater detail throughout this book.

Horizontal and vertical **scroll bars** enable you to pan your view of the active drawing.

The **drawing window** is the large white drawing surface.

The **Printable Page area** is the rectangle in the center of the Drawing window. This area represents the portion of your drawing that will print. (It is often useful to construct portions of a drawing in the Drawing window and position them in the Printable Page area later.)

The **toolbox** gives you access to the most common functions in CorelDRAW!.

The **Status line** presents you with useful information about the currently selected object.

The **rulers** are optional (they can be turned on and off from the Display menu).

The **color palette** assists you in selecting Outline and Fill colors.

Now that we are all speaking the same "language," let's look more closely at the menu bar and one of the menus it contains the **F**ile menu.

The Menu Bar

As you can see in Figure 1.2, the menu bar runs across the top of the screen, while the toolbox runs down the left-hand side. This arrangement, especially the menu bar, may strike you as familiar. As a matter of fact, all Windows applications try to maintain this arrangement.

Each menu name on the menu bar has an underlined selection letter. For example, in the **F**ile menu's name, the **F** is underlined. In this book, we show selection letters with boldface. These selection letters are used to select the menus and commands with the keyboard.

TIP: Even if you have a mouse, you might find it easier to access menus and commands with the keyboard, especially since CorelDRAW! provides many keyboard shortcuts. The procedures for opening menus and selecting commands are included here for both mouse and keyboard methods.

The following Quick Steps show how to open a menu using a mouse.

Opening a Menu with a Mouse

1. Click on the desired menu name. For example, to open the **F**ile menu, click on File.

The selected menu appears. (For example, the **F**ile menu, shown in Figure 1.3.)

NOTE: In this book, whenever you should press two keys together, we'll separate the two keys with a plus sign. For example, Alt+F means to hold down Alt while you press F.

The keyboard method for opening a menu is shown in the following Quick Steps.

Opening a Menu with the Keyboard

1. Hold down Alt and press the bold letter in the desired menu name. For example, to open the **F**ile menu, press Alt+F.

The selected menu appears. (For example, the **F**ile menu, shown in Figure 1.3.)

Notice in Figure 1.3 that there are several different ways the commands are displayed on menus. Some of the commands are grayed out, some are followed by three dots, and some have key combinations listed to the right.

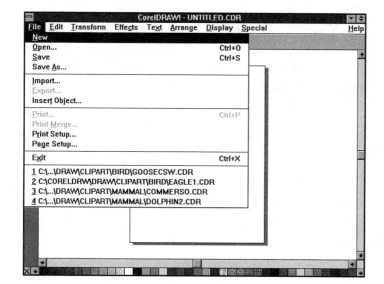

Figure 1.3
The File menu.

- Commands that are grayed out, like Export... in Figure 1.3, can't be accessed at this time. (In this case, it is because our workspace is blank and there is nothing to export.)

- Commands that are followed by three dots need more information before they can be executed. Each of these will open up another menu, called a dialog box, requesting further information. For example, the Open command requires the file name and location before the file can be opened.

- Commands that have Ctrl+ key combinations can be executed from anywhere within CorelDRAW! by pressing those keys. For example, anytime that you wish to save your work, you can press Ctrl+S.

Take a few minutes now to explore some of the menus and commands. You can't hurt anything—the worst that can happen is that you will have to restart the program.

The File Menu

If you really get into playing with the commands, you may have to clear the workspace or even restart CorelDRAW!. You'll learn how to accomplish both of these tasks in this section, as we look at the commands on the File menu (refer to Figure 1.3).

New

No great surprise here. The New command allows you to clear whatever is on the desktop and start over with a clean screen. If you have any unsaved work in process, CorelDRAW! will ask you if you wish to save it before it is erased.

Open...

As you may expect, the Open... command is used to retrieve work that has already been done or that has been saved from a previous session.

The Save command is used to store your work on a disk with the same name that it had previously been assigned.

Save As...

Save As... allows you to save your work in a different format or under a different name. This is quite useful when you wish to save several different versions of the same drawing.

Import...

Import... allows you to bring different types of art into the workspace. You can use drawings or images developed in other programs or stored in different formats.

Export...

Export... allows you to store your drawings in a format that can be used by other programs. For example, you might design a logo that you want to be able to use in a word processing or page layout program.

Object...

CorelDRAW!, as well as many of the newer Windows applications, is designed to be able to share objects created in other Windows applications. If, for example, you create a worksheet in Microsoft Excel or an equation in Microsoft Word for Windows, you can directly import it into CorelDRAW!.

Print...

With the Print... command, you can print your work on your printer or save the work to a file.

Print Merge...

Print Merge... merges text created in a word processor with the current drawing.

Print Setup...

This option lets you choose printers and printer options. This option is linked with the Printers option that you set from within the Windows Control Panel.

Page Setup

Page Setup allows you to change the paper size and orientation. You can choose a portrait or landscape page with any of several popular paper sizes—or, you can enter a custom paper size.

Exit

The **Exit** command ends the current session. If you haven't saved your work, CorelDRAW! asks you if you want to save it before you exit.

1,2,3,4

At the bottom of the **F**ile menu, the last four files that have been opened or saved are listed so you can quickly access them again.

Quitting CorelDRAW!

Had enough for one lesson? No? Then forge ahead to Chapter 2! But for those who are ready to take a break at this point, I'll explain how to quit the program.

To quit CorelDRAW!, open the File menu and choose Exit. (You can use either the keyboard or the mouse steps.) Before quitting the program, be sure to save any work that you have created or changes that you have made to an existing drawing. The following Quick Steps explain how to quit the CorelDRAW! program.

Exiting CorelDRAW!

1. Open the File menu.

2. Select Exit.   If you have not made any
                               changes, CorelDRAW! will
                               return you to the Windows
                               Program Manager. If you
                               have made changes,
                               CorelDRAW! will ask you
                               if you wish to save them.

3. If prompted, select Yes to save your changes or No to discard them.	If you choose No, CorelDRAW! will return to the Windows Program Manager, and you're finished. If you select Yes, go on to the next step
4. Enter the desired name for the drawing and select OK to save it.	CorelDRAW! will return you to the Windows Program Manager.

In this chapter, you've learned the basics and the terminology of CorelDRAW!. In Chapter 2, you will discover one of the most important learning aids available, the help system.

In This Chapter

Getting Help

Drawing a Line

Drawing Boxes, Rectangles, Circles, and Ellipses

Selecting the Object

Modifying the Object

Skewing and Rotating Objects

Getting Help on an Unselected Command

1. Press F1.
2. Select the Commands box.
3. Select the appropriate menu from the menu list.

Getting Help on a Selected Command

1. Select the menu or command with which you need help.
2. Press F1.

Getting Help by Pointing

1. Hold down the ⇧Shift key and press F1.
2. Click on the object with which you need help.

Drawing a Rectangle

1. Select the Rectangle tool from the Toolbox.
2. Position the pointer anywhere in the editing window.
3. Click and drag (move the mouse while holding down the button) to create the desired size rectangle.

Rotating and Skewing

1. Select the Rectangle tool and draw a box in the editing window.
2. Press Space bar.
3. Select the box that you drew.
4. Pick any of the arrows and drag it in the direction of the arrowhead.

Putting CorelDRAW! to Work

This chapter gets you started using some of CorelDRAW!'s powerful drawing tools. However, before you can really begin to create wonderful drawings, we will take a tour of CorelDRAW!'s most valuable feature, the Help facility.

Getting Help

One of the pleasures of CorelDRAW! is the extensive help system. Virtually any action you may want to take is covered by a help topic. The help files can be opened in several ways, the simplest of which is by pressing F1.

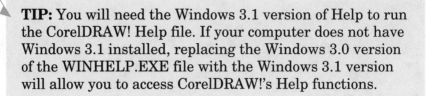

TIP: You will need the Windows 3.1 version of Help to run the CorelDRAW! Help file. If your computer does not have Windows 3.1 installed, replacing the Windows 3.0 version of the WINHELP.EXE file with the Windows 3.1 version will allow you to access CorelDRAW!'s Help functions.

For example, say you want to know what the commands in the **E**dit menu do. If your screen does not have any commands selected, the following Quick Steps show you how to find out.

Getting Help on an Unselected Command

1. Press F1.

The Help Contents screen appears.

2. Select the Commands box.

The mouse pointer changes to a pointing finger, and, when the command box is selected, a list of all the menus appears.

3. Select the appropriate menu from the list. For example, select Edit Menu.

A table of all of the Edit commands appears, along with a brief description of each command's function.

A second way to get help is to highlight a command and hold down the mouse button while pressing F1. The following Quick Steps show you how to discover what the commands in the Display menu do.

Getting Help on a Selected Command

1. Select the command that you need help with. For example, to get information about the Snap To Objects command in the **D**isplay menu, click on Display and scroll to Snap To Objects.

2. Press F1.

A window appears containing help information about the Snap To Objects command (see Figure 2.1).

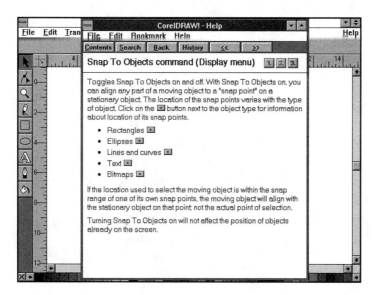

Figure 2.1
The Help screen for the Snap To Objects command.

A third way to access help is by pointing. This one is useful when you don't know the name of the object. Follow along with the example in these Quick Steps to see how the Pick tool works.

Getting Help by Pointing

1. Hold down ⇧Shift and press F1.

   The mouse pointer changes to an arrow and a question mark.

2. Place the pointer over the desired object (for example, the Pick tool, which is the first tool in the Toolbox) and click on it.

   A list of all the functions for that object appears.

There is a fourth method of obtaining help. This one is especially useful if you know the name of something and want to find out about it. For example, if you want to find out about the Bézier drawing mode, follow these Quick Steps:

Getting Help
Using Keywords

1. Select the Help menu from the menu bar.

   The Help menu appears.

2. Select Search for Keywords.

   A search dialog box appears (as shown in Figure 2.2) for the entry of the word(s) to search for.

3. Type in the keywords (for our example, Bézier drawing mode).

   Bézier drawing mode is highlighted inthe topics list.

continues

Getting Help Using Keywords *continued*

4. Press ⏎Enter.

A list of available help topics that deal with the Bézier drawing mode appears in the bottom pane of the Help window.

5. Select the desired help topic.

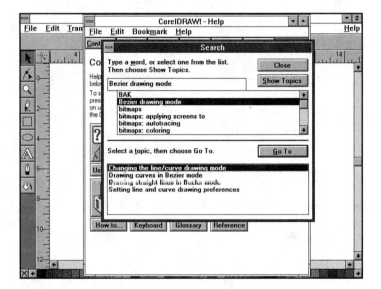

Figure 2.2

The Search for Keywords dialog box.

Play with these four different methods of obtaining help and explore the rest of the screen with them. You will find the Help function extremely valuable, both as a learning aid and as a quick refresher on skills you have already acquired.

Drawing Objects

Now it's time to put some of our newly acquired knowledge to work. Figure 2.3 points out the tools that we will be using in the rest of this chapter and in our first drawing project.

Figure 2.3
The drawing tools you will use in this book.

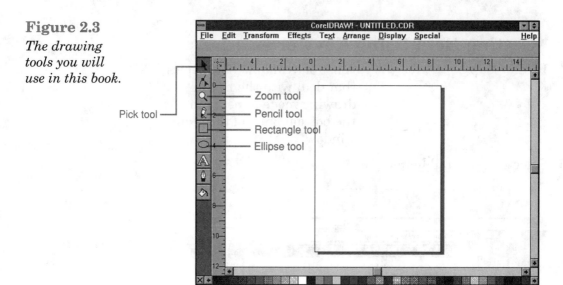

Pick tool —

(labels in figure:)
Zoom tool
Pencil tool
Rectangle tool
Ellipse tool

Drawing Lines

Let's perform a little experiment. We'll draw three different lines, using three different methods. Click on the Toolbox icon that looks like a pencil. The Pencil tool should now be selected. (If you hold the mouse button down too long, you get something called a *flyout* menu. This gives you access to Bézier curves, a topic that we will discuss in Chapter 6.)

Drawing a Freehand line: Move the mouse pointer anywhere along the left side of the editing window. Press the left mouse button and, while holding it down, attempt to draw a straight line. It could drive you over the edge, couldn't it?

Drawing a Node to Node line: With the Pencil tool selected, click and release the mouse button once. This establishes one end of the line, or node. Move the mouse about the screen, and when you have the other end of the line where you want it simply click the button again to terminate the line and establish the other node. Pretty slick, isn't it?

Drawing Constrained lines: Hold down Ctrl while you are drawing the line. Holding down the Ctrl key tells the program to keep the line straight unless the angle exceeds 15 percent, which is the default setting.

Drawing Rectangles, Squares, Ellipses, and Circles

The tool for drawing squares and rectangles and the tool for drawing circles and ellipses are located immediately below the Pencil tool (see Figure 2.3).

Both of these tools are operated by clicking and dragging to the shape desired. Follow along with these Quick Steps to draw a rectangle.

Drawing a Rectangle

1. Select the Rectangle tool.

   The icon in the Toolbox that looks like a square is highlighted.

2. Move the pointer anywhere into the editing window.

   The pointer changes into a cross hair.

3. Click and drag (move the mouse while holding down the button) to the desired size.

   A box or rectangle is drawn in the editing window.

Now, do the same thing, but with the Ellipse tool selected.

Figure 2.4 shows examples of a rectangle, an ellipse, and freehand, node to node, and constrained lines.

Figure 2.4

Lines, boxes, and circles created with drawing tools.

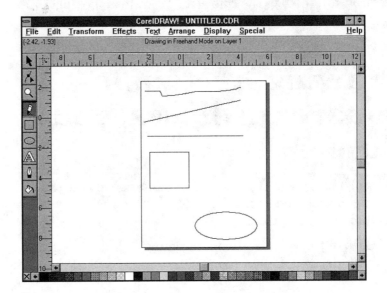

Selecting, Moving, Scaling, and Sizing Objects

As we have already discovered, the uppermost tool, the one that looks like an arrow pointing up to the left, is called the *Pick* tool. This is one of the most useful tools that you will find in the CorelDRAW! Toolbox. Click on it once and move the mouse pointer to one of the lines you just drew. While the pointer is touching the line, click once again. This selects the line so that you can manipulate it (see Figure 2.5).

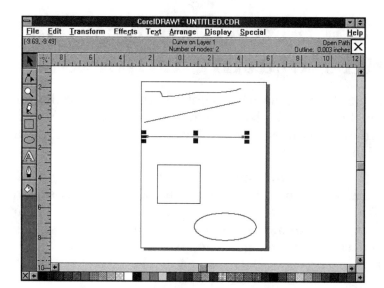

Figure 2.5
*One of the lines is
selected by using
the Pick tool.*

TIP: To quickly select the Pick tool, simply press the space bar. You can press the space bar a second time to toggle back to the tool you were using before.

There are lots of things that you can do with this line now that it is selected. First, try putting the mouse pointer on the line, pressing the mouse button and dragging the line about. You can scoot it all over the screen.

The black boxes are called *handles*. Put the mouse pointer on one of the handles that is at the end of the line, press and hold down the mouse button, and scale the line to whatever size you want. With the line still selected, press Del. This is one way to delete an object.

Now, select the square or ellipse using the Pick tool and try the same thing. Because the figure has some depth and encloses an area of space, you can make more dramatic changes in its appearance. Notice how the corner handles expand or contract the figure while maintaining its scale. And, notice that the side handles stretch or shrink the figure in one dimension.

What's Next?—Skewing and Rotating Objects

You know how to draw a line, circle, and square, as well as ellipses and rectangles. You also know how to move the object you have drawn by selecting it with the Pick tool and dragging it to a new location.

There are many times, however, when you might wish to rotate an object, or slightly distort its perspective by skewing it. To demonstrate this, first start with a clean editing window by selecting New from the File menu. When you are asked if you wish to save your changes, answer No. Then follow these Quick Steps.

Rotating and Skewing

1. Select the Rectangle tool and draw a box in the editing window.

2. Press Space bar.   The Pick tool is activated and the box is selected.

3. Click on the selected box one more time.   The box now looks like Figure 2.6.

4. Pick any of the arrows and drag it in the direction of the arrowhead.   The sets of arrows on the box's corners allow it to rotate around the center point. The sets of arrows on the box's sides allow you to skew the box.

Manipulate the box to look something like the one in Figure 2.7. Then try the following experiment.

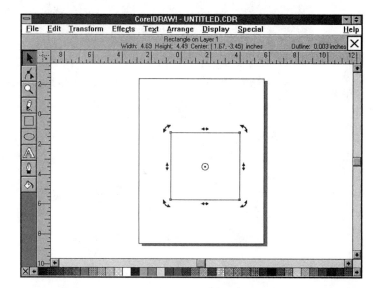

Figure 2.6

The rotating and skewing arrows.

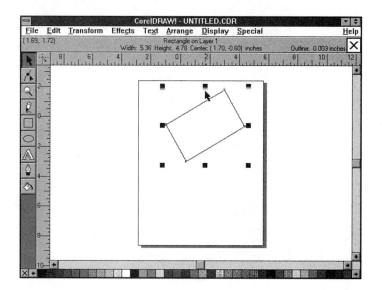

Figure 2.7

The rectangle is skewed, rotated, and selected.

Grab hold of the handle that the arrow in the figure is pointing to, and pull it down (this is the same as dragging) until your screen looks like Figure 2.8. Now let the mouse button go, and you will see that you have managed to completely flip the image vertically.

Figure 2.8

The upper middle handle has been pulled down. When the mouse botton is released, the figure will have been flipped vertically.

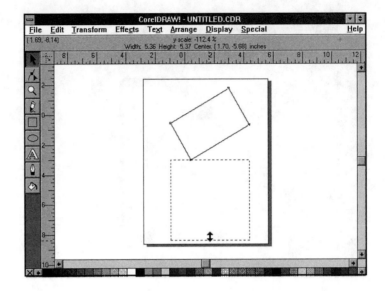

You will find a lot of use for this skill later on, especially when you are creating mirror images and special text effects.

In This Chapter

Using Rulers

Zooming In and Out

Setting Up a Grid

Using the Grid to Draw

Showing Rulers

1. Select the Display menu.
2. Select Show Rulers.

Zooming to a 1:1 Ratio

1. Select the Zoom tool (represented by a magnifying glass).
2. Select the 1:1 icon.

Constructing a 1" Grid

1. Open the File menu and select New. If you are asked to, don't save any changes.
2. Open the Display menu and select Grid Setup.
3. In the Grid Frequency box, set both Horizontal and Vertical to 1.00 per inch.
4. Select Show Grid and Snap To Grid.
5. Select OK.

Zooms, Rulers, and Grids

We have already learned a great deal about CorelDRAW!. Looking back, we now know how to draw lines, circles, and rectangles. We can rotate and skew them, as well as move them around in the editing window.

For those of us who like to be precise, CorelDRAW! provides some professional-quality positioning aids, such as rulers, a zoom feature, and an adjustable grid. In this chapter we will learn how to use them.

Using Rulers

CorelDRAW!'s rulers can be either hidden or visible, whichever you prefer. The first time you use the program, they'll be hidden. Since the position of the rulers is saved from session to session, the measurements on your rulers may not be identical to those shown in the figures. You will learn how to modify the rulers later in this chapter.

For the exercises in this book, you'll want the rulers to be visible. If your rulers are not on the screen, choose Show Rulers from the Display menu. The following Quick Steps summarize this easy procedure.

Showing Rulers

1. Select the Display menu.   The Display menu opens.

2. Select Show Rulers.   The rulers appear. If you were to pull down the Display menu again, you'd see a checkmark beside Show Rulers.

Your screen should now look like the one in Figure 3.1.

Figure 3.1

The rulers are displayed.

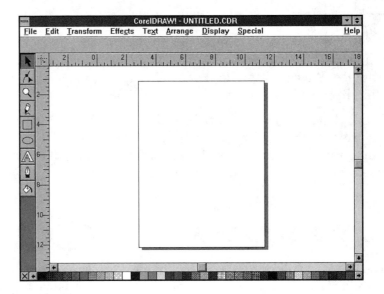

TIP: If the measurements on your rulers are not in inches, you can change them in the Grid Frequency section of the Grid Setup dialog box. Select Grid Setup from the Display menu and change the Grid Frequency settings to read 16 per inch (or any other number up to 72) for both Horizontal and Vertical measurements. If you ever have the occasion to measure in millimeters, picas, or points, this is where you would change the markings on the rulers.

Changing the Zero Points of the Rulers

Rulers are of the most use when you can start measuring at zero. If you were limited to using the ruler as it appears in Figure 3.1, you could easily spend as much time with a pocket calculator figuring out line lengths as you would spend drawing. Let's take care of that.

Where the two rulers come together in the upper left hand corner of the Editing Window, right next to the Pick tool, is an icon that looks like a cross with an arrow pointing down and to the right. This is called the ruler cross hairs icon. Put your mouse pointer on this icon and drag it into the Editing Window (see Figure 3.2). When you release the mouse button, the zero points of the rulers will move to the new location.

TIP: The status bar—the area immediately below the menu bar—contains a lot of useful information. The numbers in parentheses indicate the location of the pointer. The first number is how far the pointer is away from zero on the horizontal axis, and the second gives you the same information on the vertical axis. You can obtain measurements accurate to 1/100 of an inch by placing the zero point at one end of a line and moving the pointer to the other. The status bar will tell you how long the line is.

Figure 3.2

Dragging ruler origins into the Editing Window.

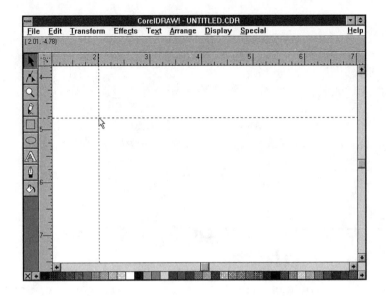

Zooming the Display

It would be quite difficult to draw a line or figure with any great precision, say to the nearest 1/16th or 1/72nd of an inch, with the scale of the editing window as it now appears. Follow along while we change this scale to 1:1, or *WYSIWYG*. (Pronounced "whiz-i-wig," it means What You See Is What You Get.) In WYSIWYG mode, the image on the screen is actual size, the same size as that which will be printed.

QUICK STEPS

Zooming to a 1:1 Ratio

1. Select the Zoom tool (represented by a magnifying glass).

   A flyout menu opens showing the zooming options.

2. Select the 1:1 (Actual Size) icon.

   The Editing Window and the rulers zoom in to become actual size (see Figure 3.3).

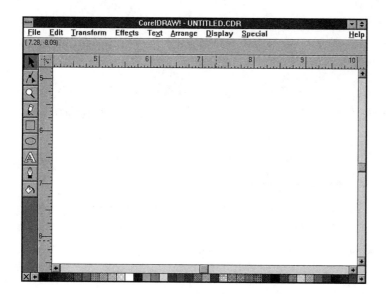

Figure 3.3
The screen is shown at actual size when 1:1 is selected.

To Zoom In, you select the plus magnifying glass from the tool's flyout menu; the cursor changes into the form of the icon. There are two ways to use this tool. The first is to simply position the cursor over the area you wish to Zoom In on and click the mouse button. This will magnify the area by a factor of two.

The second way is to select the plus magnifying glass icon and drag a box around the object or area you wish to magnify. This will expand the area within the box to use the full screen.

The other icons on the flyout menu are even easier to use and understand, since selecting the icon accomplishes its function without further work on your part. The Zoom Out icon, the minus magnifying glass, will reduce the drawing by a factor of two or return you to the view you had prior to your last Zoom In.

The Fit in Window icon will bring into view all the objects in the drawing, zooming in or out at whatever magnification is necessary to accomplish this. The Show Page icon will display the entire printable page in the editing window.

Experiment with the various Zoom tools—you will be using all of them frequently.

TIP: Don't be afraid to change the position of the rulers and the magnification often. You can measure lines precisely by placing a zero point on one end of the line, increasing magnification, and reading from the ruler. The changes will not have any effect on your artwork.

Memory Joggers

One of the most important things you can learn is how to "remember" what you learned.

For example, you know that we have talked about the Zoom tool before, but you aren't sure you really understand what it does.

Remember this key sequence: ⟨⇧Shift⟩+⟨F1⟩. This will change your pointer into a question mark and an arrow. If you point at the Zoom tool and click the mouse button, you will see the help screen shown in Figure 3.4.

Figure 3.4

The Zoom tool Help screen.

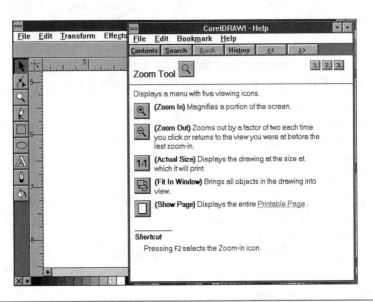

Drawing Using a Grid

If you have the Snap to Grid option turned on, the grid can act as a series of very strong magnets running horizontally and vertically in the Editing Window. Any line that you draw is attracted to the closest magnet, and snaps into place. This is demonstrated in the following Quick Steps.

Constructing a Grid

1. Open the File menu and select New. If you're asked to, do not save any changes.	A new Editing Window appears.
2. Open the Display menu and select Grid Setup.	The Grid Setup dialog box appears (see Figure 3.5).
3. In the Grid Frequency box, set both Horizontal and Vertical to 1.00 per inch.	
4. Select Show Grid and Snap To Grid.	
5. Select OK.	The Editing Window appears with the grid visible (represented by dots). The status bar contains the reminder that Snap to Grid is turned on.

You would seldom use a grid with so much space between points. However, our first project will show the power of the Snap to Grid feature.

Figure 3.5

The Grid Setup dialog box.

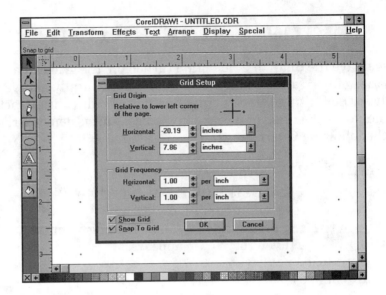

Project 1—Geometric Art

Now let's test the grid feature by creating something. The figure that we're going to create in the following steps will also be used in the next chapter, when you learn about printing and saving your work.

1. Select the Zoom tool and select its 1:1 icon.

2. Locate your zero points in the same general area as those shown in Figure 3.6.

3. Be sure your Grid Setup dialog box looks like Figure 3.5. Grid frequency should be 1.00 inches for both horizontal and vertical, and the Show Grid and Snap To Grid boxes should be checked.

4. Select the Rectangle tool and draw a box that is five inches wide by three inches deep. Use the status bar's position numbers to do this. Click at point (0.00, 0.00) and drag down and to the right until the status bar shows you are at point (5.00, -3.00). Notice how the box "snaps" from grid point to grid point.

5. Select the Ellipse tool.

6. Click in the upper left corner of the box and drag the oval down to the lower right corner.

7. Select the Pencil tool.

8. Draw two diagonal lines from corner to corner by clicking once on each end point of the line.

9. Draw a horizontal line one inch down from the top of your figure.

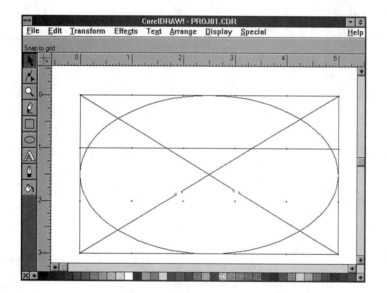

Figure 3.6
*Project 1—
geometric art.*

What's Next?—Using Wireframe View

You have already learned that draw programs, like CorelDRAW!, keep track of your drawing by storing the equations that make up the lines and curves. This, as you may imagine, can put quite a strain on your computer, especially when it is calculating some of the very complex equations that are associated with the special effects we will learn about in later chapters.

The first clue you will have that your computer is working hard will be a delay in drawing your art work on the computer monitor. You can simplify the computer's task, without sacrificing quality, by telling the computer to only display the outlines of a drawing. The computer will still keep track of color, fills and other attributes, but it will not display them. This is called Wireframe view. To turn Wireframe editing on or off, simply select Edit Wireframe from the Display menu or press ⇧Shift+F9.

In this chapter you have learned some of the basics about drawing. Chapter 4 will show how CorelDRAW! saves your drawings and prints them.

In This Chapter

Saving a Drawing for the First Time

Saving an Existing Drawing

Setting Print Options

Printing a Drawing

Using Keywords and Notes

Saving a Drawing for the First Time

1. Open the File menu.
2. Select Save.
3. If necessary, change the drive and/or directory.
4. Type a name for your drawing.
5. Select OK.

Saving an Existing Drawing

1. Open the File menu.
2. Select Save.

Printing a Drawing

1. Open the File menu.
2. Select Print.
3. Make any print option selections.
4. Select OK.

Saving and Printing

In the last chapter, we created a drawing out of some lines and shapes on the grid. But a drawing is not much good unless you have some way of getting it off your screen and into a form that other people can admire! So this chapter will focus on printing and saving, two excellent ways to share your artistry with others.

Saving a File

Your first piece of art is now finished, or is it? How are you going to show this to your spouse, keep it for eventual display at the Smithsonian, or store it so we can use it later, if it hasn't been saved?

The following Quick Steps explain how to save a file.

Saving a Drawing for the First Time

1. Open the File menu.	The File pull-down menu appears.
2. Select Save.	Since the file has never been saved before, the Save Drawing dialog box appears (see Figure 4.1).
3. If necessary, change the drive and/or directory.	
4. Type a name for your drawing. For our example, call it proj01.cdr.	
5. Select OK.	The file is saved.

Figure 4.1

The Save Drawing dialog box.

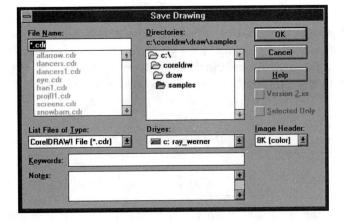

If you want to preserve the original version of a file and save the new version, too, use Save As from the File menu. Save As brings back the Save Drawing dialog box, where you can specify a new name.

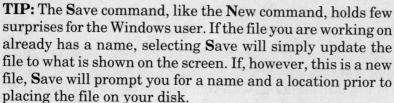

TIP: The **S**ave command, like the **N**ew command, holds few surprises for the Windows user. If the file you are working on already has a name, selecting **S**ave will simply update the file to what is shown on the screen. If, however, this is a new file, **S**ave will prompt you for a name and a location prior to placing the file on your disk.

Saving an Existing Drawing

QUICK STEPS

1. Open the File menu.

2. Select Save.

Since the file already has a name, CorelDRAW! saves it without further information.

CAUTION

Be careful when using the **S**ave command on an existing drawing. Saving a file with the same name will entirely replace the old version with the new one. If you aren't quite sure whether or not you will ever want to see that old version again, use Save **A**s instead.

Getting Ready to Print

The whole idea behind CorelDRAW! is to create work that can be printed. You may want to either print it on your own printer or save the print output in a file that can be sent to a service bureau, another artist, or a friend.

If you were using Windows with printers before you bought CorelDRAW!, you're ready to go. Just use the printers you've already installed. Since all Windows programs share a common printer driver, CorelDRAW! can use it, too.

Setting up to use a friend's printer requires that you know what kind of printer the friend has, and then install a driver for it on your system (see your Windows documentation).

Setting up a printer driver to be used with a service bureau can be a simple procedure, or it can be an arduous one requiring technical conversations with your service bureau. It just depends on what their requirements are. (Don't worry overly much about this—if someone wants your business, they will be sure that you can save/print your work in a format that they can use.)

Changing Print Options

To access the Print Setup dialog box shown in Figure 4.2, follow these steps:

1. Open the File menu.

2. Select Print Setup.

From this dialog box, you can choose one of the installed printers and set the paper orientation and size.

Figure 4.2

The Print Setup dialog box.

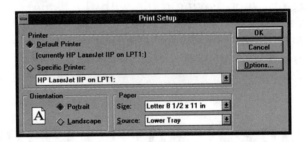

You can select the Options button to control specific features unique to your printer. For example, on most laser printers, you can control print intensity (darkness) and dithering (the way the printer prints patterns and colors). Figure 4.3 shows the available options for a Linotronic 300 PostScript printer.

When you're finished making changes, select OK to close the dialog boxes and return to your editing window.

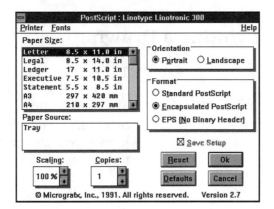

Figure 4.3
Available options for a Linotronic 300 PostScript printer.

Printing a Drawing

Printing your work can be a very simple exercise. When you select Print, a dialog box offers some basic options (which differ depending on the type of printer). Select the ones you want, and go! For a summary, just follow these Quick Steps.

Printing a Drawing

1. Open the File menu.

2. Select Print.

   A Print Options dialog box will appear. The options it contains will depend on the type of printer selected (see Figures 4.4 and 4.5).

3. Make any desired changes to the print options.

   Use the Help menu with the pointer, ⇧Shift + F1 , to explore the various options. (See Figure 4.6.)

   continues

Printing a Drawing *continued*

4. Select OK.

The portion of the drawing that is in the Printable Page area of the editing window is printed. (If your drawing is larger than the printable page, you will have to use the Fit to Page or Scale options in the print options dialog box.)

Figure 4.4

The Print Options dialog box for a Non-PostScript printer.

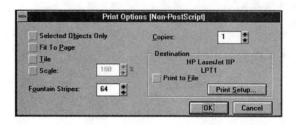

Figure 4.5

The Print Options dialog box for a PostScript printer.

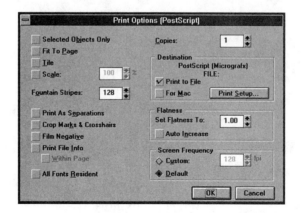

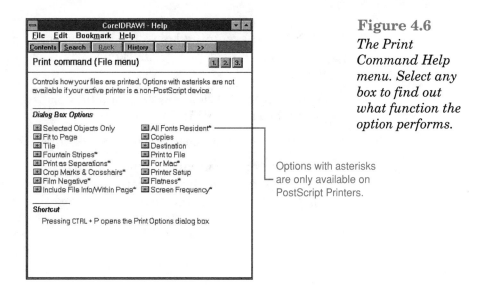

Figure 4.6
The Print Command Help menu. Select any box to find out what function the option performs.

What's Next?— Keywords and Notes

Keywords and *Notes* are two very useful options available to you when saving files. You may remember that when we discussed opening a drawing, there was an area in the Open Drawing dialog box that allowed us to find drawings by using keywords. These keywords can be assigned when the file is saved.

Keywords give you a quick way to access a particular drawing, or a related group of drawings. Say, for instance, that you have been assigned to develop a group of drawings revolving about the theme of teddy bears engaging in water sports. You have developed a piece of art that shows a mama bear taking a water ski jump. You could then assign the following keywords:

```
bear project,mama bear,water ski,ski jump,crash.
```

The *Notes* area gives you a great way to keep track of the history of an individual piece of art. If you keep track of each time a particular drawing is used, you will avoid the not uncommon mistake of using the same drawing several times within a short time frame.

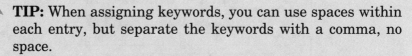

TIP: When assigning keywords, you can use spaces within each entry, but separate the keywords with a comma, no space.

As a matter of style, keywords should be assigned from the general to the specific. For example:

```
bear project,mama bear,water ski,ski jump,crash
```

In this example you can search for all drawings related to the bear project, those that just contain mama bear, those relating to water skiing, and so on.

In This Chapter

Opening a File

Using the Outline Tool

Grouping Objects

Duplicating Objects

Creating Mirror Images

Object Alignment

Opening a File

1. Open the File menu.
2. Select Open.
3. Select the desired filename from the listing.
4. Select OK.

Opening the Outline Pen Roll-Up Window

1. Select the Pen tool.
2. Select the second button in the top row of the Outline Tool's flyout menu.

Applying Color to Outlines

1. Select the Outline Pen tool.
2. Select the Outline Pen Roll-Up window icon.
3. Use the Pick tool to select the rectangle.
4. Select the line thickness and line style desired, then click on the color selector bar.
5. Select the color desired.
6. Select the Apply box.
7. Save your work by pressing Ctrl+S$$$.

Grouping Your Drawing

1. Open the Edit menu and choose Select All.
2. Open the Arrange menu and select Group.
3. Save your work.

Duplicating an Object or Group of Objects

1. Select the object or group to be duplicated.
2. Open the Edit menu and select Duplicate, or press Ctrl+D.
3. Drag the duplicate to its new position.

Jazzing Up
the Line

In this chapter, we will continue working on proj01.cdr. Unfortunately, we left our project in a rather boring state—all of its lines were of the same thickness and weight, and it wasn't awfully appealing. We will go a long way toward fixing those faults in this chapter.

Reopening the Drawing

The first thing you need to do is to reopen the proj01.cdr file (unless it's already open). Follow these Quick Steps to do so:

Opening a File

1. Open the File menu.

2. Select Open.   The Open Drawing dialog
                                    box appears.

3. Select the desired filename from the listing.
   For our example, choose
   `proj01.cdr`.

4. Select OK.   The file is opened.

The Outline Pen

The Outline Pen carries that name for obvious reasons. Use this tool to vary the line size, color, and appearance of the lines that outline your work.

TIP: If your lines don't take on any depth or refuse to change colors or dimensions, you may be in Wireframe View mode. Hold down ⇧Shift and press F9. This key combination toggles Wireframe on and off.

The Outline Pen tool looks like a fountain pen. Click on it, and you will get a flyout menu that looks like Figure 5.1. The upper row gives you some basic line sizes. Starting from the right to left, Corel has provided us with Real Fat, Fat, Normal, Thin, Skinny, and None (represented by a bold X).

Figure 5.1
*The Outline Pen's
flyout menu.*

TIP: If you are wondering why you are given a none option, remember that this is the outline tool. There may be instances where you don't want a figure outlined in black, or any other color for that matter.

Select the rectangle in proj01 by selecting the Pick tool and then clicking on one of its sides. Now click on each of the line size boxes on the flyout menu to see what happens. Notice that on the status bar, the line size is shown in fractions of an inch after the word Outline.

Opening the Pen Roll-Up Window

I am sure that you'll be satisfied with the Outline Pen's flyout menu, but having access to only four different line sizes is very limiting. Fortunately, you have more options. Follow these Quick Steps to see the Pen Roll-Up window.

Opening the Pen Roll-Up Window

1. Select the Pen tool.	The Outline Pen's flyout menu opens.
2. Select the second button in the top row of the Outline tool's flyout menu.	The Pen Roll-Up window opens (see Figure 5.2).

Figure 5.2
The Pen Roll-Up window.

Just what you need, another menu. This kind of menu is called a *Roll-Up window* because it will operate just like a window shade.

The upper right corner of the new window has an arrow. Click on the arrow once to roll the shade up, and once again to roll it down. You can drag this window anywhere within the editing window that is convenient.

More Line Thickness Control

Directly under the Pen Roll-Up window's title bar is the *thickness selector*. With it, you may select lines as thin as 1/4 of a point size or as thick as 24 points. The selector box contains a cross hair and arrows pointing up and down.

To test this feature, do the following:

1. Select the oval in proj01 by using the Pick tool.

2. In the thickness selector box, click repeatedly on the up arrow until you get the desired thickness.

3. Select Apply to see the results (shown in Figure 5.3).

As you can see, this box gives you complete control over the width of your outlines. The up arrow increases the line's thickness; the down arrow decreases it.

Adding Arrows to Lines

Let's move down one more box in the roll-up window, to the *arrowhead selectors*. The two lines in separate compartments represent the ends of any lines you may draw. Say, perhaps, that you would like the left side of a line to have an arrow that points to something. Click on the left box and see how many options you have! Now try the right side.

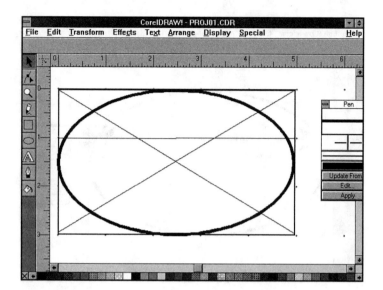

Figure 5.3
The oval now appears thicker.

NOTE: Whenever you make changes in the Pen Roll-Up window, the changes will not take effect until you select the Apply button.

For the purposes of our project, try the following:

1. Select the straight line that runs horizontally across the project.

2. Click on the box that represents each end of the line and attach an arrowhead, the third one on the top row.

3. Select a line thickness.

4. Select Apply to put your changes into effect (see Figure 5.4).

Figure 5.4

The horizontal line now has an arrowhead at each end.

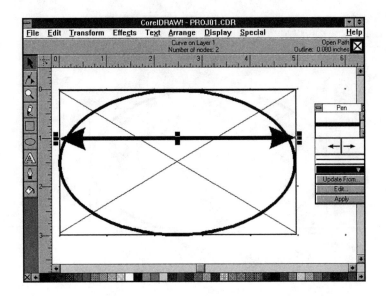

Dotted or Dashed Lines

Straight lines can be fun, but there are many instances where you may want a dotted or dashed line. The next box down in the Pen Roll-Up window, the *line style selector*, depicts a line. Click on it and see how many options CorelDRAW! gives you!

Now, to keep up with the project, follow these steps:

1. Select the straight line that has the arrowheads on each end.

2. Click on the line box in the Roll-Up window to display the line choices.

3. Select the first dashed line.

4. Select Apply to make the change take effect (see Figure 5.5).

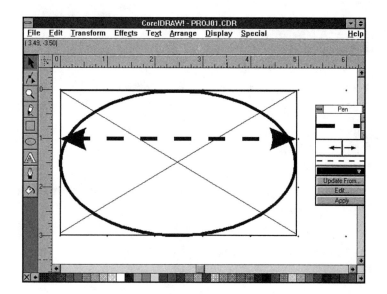

Figure 5.5

*The line now
appears dashed.*

Changing Outline Color

I think that you will enjoy the next box the most. This box looks
like a black bar with a little triangle inside it. It's used to change
the color of outlines. Follow along with these Quick Steps to see
how it is used.

Applying Color to Outlines

1. Select the Outline Pen
   tool.

   The Outline flyout menu
   opens.

2. Select the Pen Roll-Up
   window icon.

   The Pen Roll-Up window
   opens in the editing window.

3. Use the Pick tool to
   select the rectangle.

   The rectangle becomes
   selected, and its handles
   become visible.

   continues

Applying Color to Outlines *continued*

4. Click on the color selector.

A palette of outline colors is displayed (see Figure 5.6).

5. Select the color desired (for our example, choose red).

The color selector bar and the thickness selector change colors.

6. Select Apply.

The rectangle assumes the thickness, line style, and color selected.

7. Save your work by pressing Ctrl+S.

Saving will update proj01.cdr to reflect the changes we have made.

Figure 5.6

The outline color selection palette.

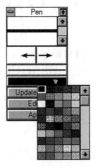

Advanced Color Selection

Let's look at the Edit button on the Pen Roll-Up window. When you select it, you will see the Outline Pen dialog box shown in Figure 5.7, which allows you to change all line attributes in one handy location. This dialog box also gives you access to some options not available elsewhere—in particular, additional colors.

Modern computers are quite capable of displaying over 25 million different colors. As extensive as the palette under the pen menu is, it provides us with a far from complete selection.

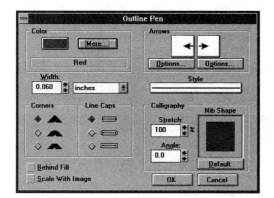

Figure 5.7
*The Outline Pen
dialog box.*

If you click on the Color box, you will see the same selections you had before. However, click on the More button. Depending upon the capabilities of your computer and monitor, you now have access to the entire spectrum of colors that can be shown, in either process or spot color modes.

Since it is not the place of a *First Book* to delve into great detail about the differences in the various types and modes of color, at this point, you only need to know that they are there. Play with the colors, select them, and see how those selections change your work.

NOTE: The Arrows boxes in the Outline Pen dialog box look familiar, and they are—with one major exception. If you can't find just the right arrow, you can select one that is close and then edit it. If you select any of the arrow ends, and then select Options, you will be presented with the choices **N**one, **S**wap, **E**dit, and **D**elete From List. Selecting Edit allows you to change the appearance of the arrow.

Using Your New Skills

Using the procedures you have learned, select each of the diagonal lines, give them some thickness, and color them blue.

Did you forget to change the line ends back to blank? No problem: choose the arrowhead selectors and click on the very first icon, a line with no arrow. Do this for both ends and apply it to each diagonal line. Your work should now look like that in Figure 5.8. Use the Ctrl+S key combination to save your work.

Figure 5.8

Project proj01.cdr.

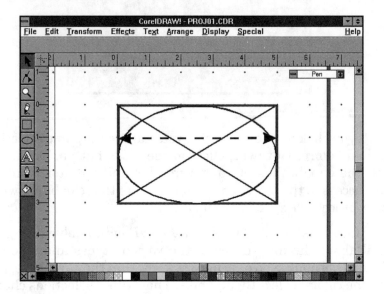

Grouping Objects

Our project—as pretty as it is becoming—is still a series of separate and distinct shapes. We really don't want it to remain that way. Say, for example, that we were drawing a ladder. The ladder may have rungs and rails as components, but when we lean it up against a house, we want the whole ladder to move as a unit.

CorelDRAW! gives us the ability to *group* or combine many separate objects and treat them all as one unit. That's what we'll do with our project, as shown in the following Quick Steps.

Grouping a Drawing

1. Open the Edit menu and choose Select All.

   All objects are selected and the status bar reads `5 objects selected on Layer 1`.

2. Open the Arrange menu and select Group.

   The objects have become Grouped and the status bar reads `Group of 5 objects on Layer 1`.

3. Save your work by pressing `Ctrl`+`S`.

Grouping is a reversible process. If you later decide that you want to modify an object within this group, you could simply select the group and choose Ungroup from the Arrange menu.

Grouping Selected Objects

The method of grouping objects just described works well if everything in the editing window is to be grouped. There are, however, two additional ways to select objects to be grouped.

1. *Picking individual objects:* To group several objects that are not all in the same area or have other objects between them, you can use the Pick tool. With the Pick tool selected you can hold down the `Shift` key while clicking on the objects you wish to be grouped. You can then group the objects by pressing `Ctrl`+`G`.

2. *Selecting an area to be grouped:* To select a particular area of a drawing to be grouped, first select the Pick tool. Then move to one corner of the area, and, while holding down the mouse button, drag the pointer to the opposite corner.

A rubber band box traces around the area, and the objects are selected. You can then group the objects by pressing Ctrl + G.

Scaling, Duplicating, and Mirroring

Imagine that you think this graphic we have created is the best thing since God made trees. As a matter of fact, you love it so much that you want to make *wallpaper* out of it, or *tile* a series of the image. There are only a couple of problems: first, it would be nice to include an element that mirrored what we have done; and second, you have better things to do with your day than draw hundreds of identical objects.

Scaling

Let's start by scaling our graphic down to 4 inches wide by 2 inches deep.

Scaling an Object or Group

1. Select the object or group that you want to scale.

    Handles appear.

2. Drag any one of the corner handles to the desired size. Zoom in and out and reposition the rulers as necessary.

    The rulers and the numbers on the Status line serve as guides.

Open the Zoom tool flyout menu and select the Show Page option (the last one in the line). Now drag the graphic into the upper left-hand corner of the Printable Page area, so it looks like Figure 5.9.

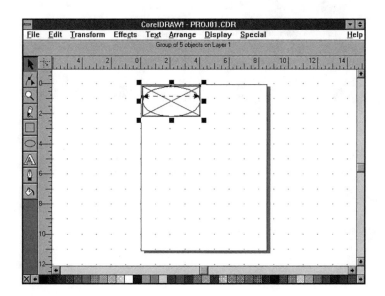

Figure 5.9
*Graphic positioned
for duplication.*

Duplicating

Next, we'll duplicate our drawing so that the page is covered with
small, identical objects. Follow these Quick Steps to learn how.

Duplicating an Object or Group

QUICK STEPS

1. Select object or group to
   be duplicated.

   Handles appear around the
   selected object or group.

2. Select **D**uplicate from
   the **E**dit menu, or press
   Ctrl+D.

   An exact duplicate of the
   object or group is created.

3. Drag the duplicate to its
   new position.

Zoom in and position the graphics as they are in Figure 5.10.

Figure 5.10

Graphics duplicated and positioned to mirror.

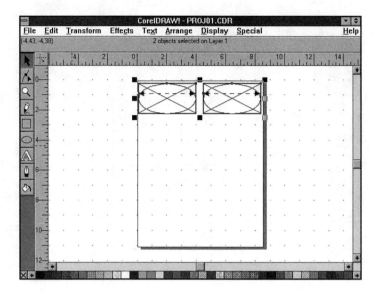

Mirroring and Making Wallpaper

1. Select the Pick tool.

2. Hold down the ⇧Shift key and click on each of the two graphics. Or, choose Select All from the Edit menu.

   As each object is selected, it is added to a new group.

3. Open the Transform menu.

   The pull-down menu opens.

4. Select Stretch & Mirror.

   The Stretch & Mirror dialog box opens (see Figure 5.11).

5. Check the Leave Original box.

6. Select Vert Mirror.

7. Select OK.

A duplicate, mirrored along the vertical axis, appears directly on top of the original.

8. Drag the mirrored group to a position below the original.

Four graphics now appear in the Printable Page area.

9. Repeat steps 1 through 8 using all four graphics.

When you've done all four, the wallpaper will look like Figure 5.12.

10. Save your work.

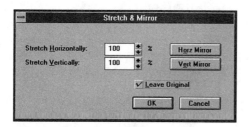

Figure 5.11

The Stretch and Mirror Dialog Box.

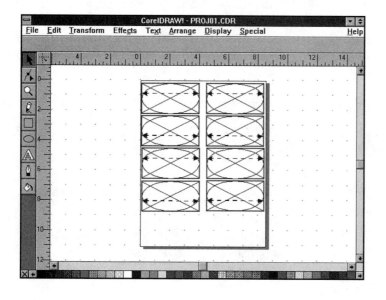

Figure 5.12

The completed project.

TIP: As you duplicate your figure, you might find it helpful to have your Snap to Grid option activated (it's in the Display menu, or use the keyboard shortcut Ctrl+Y), and your grid setup set to 10 per inch, horizontal and vertical.

What's Next?—More on Object Alignment

You know how easy it is to drag images into position, but it is very difficult to be precise when using the mouse. There are three different ways to align objects within CorelDRAW!. One of them is to use the Snap to Grid feature, with which you are already familiar. The other two, guidelines and nudging, will be discussed here.

Guidelines

The easiest way to think about guidelines is to consider them as individual, moveable gridlines. You can position them anywhere in the editing window and instruct objects to snap to them in exactly the same way that you can with gridlines. The following Quick Steps show how to set up guidelines.

Establishing Horizontal and Vertical Guidelines

1. Open the File menu and select New.

   A blank editing window opens.

2. With the rulers visible, drag the origin point to the upper left corner of the Printable Page area.

   The zero points of the rulers are positioned.

3. Click anywhere on the left ruler, and drag the pointer into the editing window.	A vertical guideline is created.
4. Click anywhere on the top ruler, and drag the pointer into the editing window.	A horizontal guideline is created.
5. Drag the guidelines into the desired position.	
6. Select Snap to Guidelines from the Display menu.	The guidelines are activated.

Nudging

You can use the directional arrows on the keyboard to position selected objects with great precision. This process is called *nudging*, and the amount that an object is nudged, or moved, with each keypress can be adjusted in the Preferences dialog box. The following Quick Steps demonstrate nudging.

Changing the Nudge Measurement

1. Open the Special menu and select Preferences. Or press Ctrl+J.	The Preferences dialog box opens.
2. Change the measurement in the Nudge box (for example, to 0.05 inches) and select OK.	The measurement is changed.

Each keypress on one of the directional arrows will now move a selected object or group of objects the specified amount (for example, 0.05 inch) in the direction of the arrow.

In this chapter you have become familiar with the use of basic geometric shapes and modifying their appearance and alignment by using some of the tools of CorelDRAW!. Chapter 6 will expand on what you have learned by introducing the technique of drawing curves, circles, and segments.

In This Chapter

Curving a Straight Line

Drawing in Freehand Mode

Drawing in Bézier Mode

Using the Shape Tool

Selecting the Freehand or Bézier Tool

1. Place the mouse cursor on the Pencil tool and hold down the mouse button until a flyout menu appears.
2. Select the Freehand tool or the Bézier tool.

Drawing Curves in Freehand Mode

1. Select the Freehand tool.
2. With the cursor in the editing window, hold down the mouse button and draw.
3. Release the button when you're finished.

Drawing Curves in Bézier Mode

1. Select the Bézier tool.
2. Position the cursor where you want the curve to start.
3. Press and hold the mouse button.
4. Drag in the direction that you want the curve to be drawn.
5. Release the mouse button.
6. Position the cursor where you want the curve to end.
7. Press and hold the mouse button.
8. Drag in the direction that you want the curve to be drawn.
9. Repeat as needed.

Shaping a Curve

1. Select the Bézier tool and draw a series of curves.
2. Select the Shape tool.
3. Select one of the nodes.
4. Shape the curve by dragging the control points.
5. Drag the selected node to another location.

Drawing Curves, Circles, and Segments

Up until now you have been more or less stuck with straight lines. In this chapter we will learn how to curve and shape lines into more useful configurations.

Curving a Straight Line

There are three separate methods of curving lines:

- Drawing freehand
- Using the Bézier tool
- Using the Shape tool

Each has its advantages and limitations. You might, for example, choose to draw freehand when tweaking a piece of clip art or performing a task that requires little precision. The Bézier tool will give you the ability to draw with much greater exactness. The Shape tool is in a class by itself, allowing great precision as well as many other features.

Both Freehand and Bézier mode are accessed through the Pencil tool's flyout menu. Follow these Quick Steps to access them.

Selecting the Freehand or Bézier Tool

1. Place the mouse cursor on the Pencil tool and hold down the mouse button until a flyout menu appears.

   The pencil tool flyout menu appears (see Figure 6.1). The left tool is Freehand; the right tool is Bézier.

2. Select the Freehand tool or the Bézier tool.

   The status bar reads Drawing in Freehand Mode or Drawing in Bézier Mode.

Figure 6.1
The Pencil tool flyout menu.

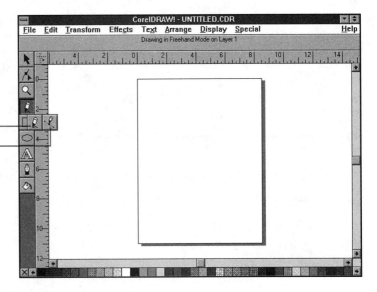

Freehand tool ———

Bézier tool ———

Drawing Freehand

Now that you know how to select the Freehand tool, you're ready to draw a freehand curve. Follow these Quick Steps to do so.

Drawing Curves in Freehand Mode

1. Select the Freehand tool.

2. With the cursor in the editing window, hold down the mouse button and draw.

   A line appears where the cursor has been dragged.

3. Release the button when you're finished.

   CorelDRAW! calculates the path of the curve you have drawn and redraws it with a smoother appearance.

TIP: To erase part of the line or curve that you are drawing, hold down ⇧Shift while continuing to drag back over the path you want to remove. When you release ⇧Shift, you will be able to resume your drawing.

If you want to draw a second line or curve that is connected to the first, continue with the freehand pencil and start your drag from the endpoint of the last segment.

Drawing in Bézier Mode

Nodes and control points are the building blocks of drawing curves in CorelDRAW! (see Figure 6.2). Here are some terms that you need to know before going any further:

- *Nodes:* Boxes along the path of a curve that anchor the Control Points.

- *Control Points:* These determine the angle that a curve takes on when it passes through a Node.

- *Segments:* The part of a curve that is between two nodes.

Figure 6.2

Nodes, control points, and segments.

Control point ———

Node ———

Segment ———

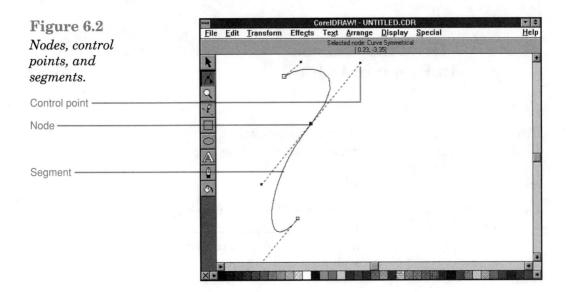

When you select the Bézier tool, Drawing in Bézier mode will appear in the status bar.

The Bézier tool can be used to draw straight lines exactly like the Freehand one: just click once for each end of the line. However, the real power of this tool is displayed when drawing curves.

Now, let's draw a Bézier curve. Follow these Quick Steps.

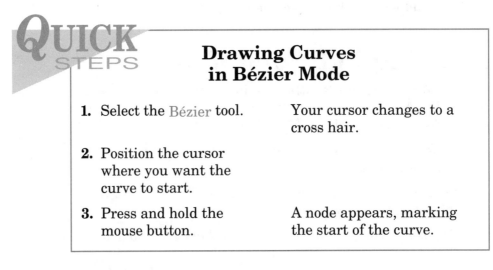

Drawing Curves in Bézier Mode

1. Select the Bézier tool.

   Your cursor changes to a cross hair.

2. Position the cursor where you want the curve to start.

3. Press and hold the mouse button.

   A node appears, marking the start of the curve.

4. Drag in the direction that you want the curve to be drawn.	Two control points will move in opposite directions from the node.
5. Release the mouse button.	
6. Position the cursor where you want the curve to end.	
7. Press and hold the mouse button.	A node appears, marking the end of the curve.
8. Drag in the direction that you want the curve to be drawn.	Two control points will move in opposite directions from the node.
9. Repeat as needed.	

You may have noticed a couple of things about drawing in the Bézier mode. The first is that the control points determine the height and slope of the curve. The slope is adjusted by dragging the control points around the node, while the height of the slope is determined by dragging the control points closer to, or away from, the node.

Additionally, you discovered that curve segments automatically join together, as long as you keep adding nodes. You can disable this by pressing the space bar twice before you define the next starting point.

Let's leave the curve and learn about the Shape tool. When you come back, you will be prepared to do some pretty amazing things with your curve.

Using the Shape Tool

You already know that you can stretch, move, scale, skew, and mirror objects by using the Pick tool. All of these functions change the object, but they leave its basic shape intact. The Shape tool, however, allows you to change the basic shape of an object.

The icon for this tool is the second from the top in the Toolbox. It looks something like a collapsing teeter-totter. The operation of this tool varies for each object type, so follow along with these Quick Steps as we change the shape of rectangles and ellipses.

Shaping a Rectangle

1. Select the Rectangle tool and draw a rectangle in the editing window.

2. Select the Shape tool.   The cursor changes into an arrow point.

3. Select the rectangle.   The four corners (nodes) appear.

4. Drag any one of the nodes along the lines of the rectangle.   The corners become rounded.

Notice that the status bar displays the corner radius of the rectangle.

Shaping an Ellipse

1. Select the Ellipse tool and draw an ellipse in the editing window.

2. Select the Shape tool.   The cursor changes into an arrow point.

3. Select the ellipse.   A node appears.

4. Drag the nodes around the perimeter of the ellipse.	An arc is created if you drag outside of the ellipse, or a wedge is created if you drag around the inside of the ellipse.

Your modified rectangle and ellipse will look similar to the ones in Figure 6.3. Notice that the status bar displays the angle of the nodes at either end of the arc, as well as the total angle of the arc. The word "distorted" means that the arc is not taken from a perfect circle.

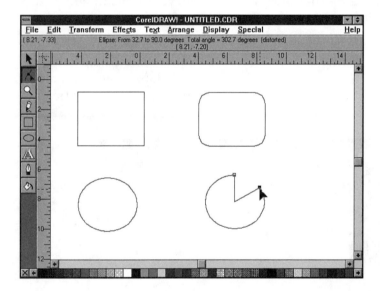

Figure 6.3
A Rectangle and an Ellipse after being shaped.

Shaping Lines and Curves

The Shape tool can be used to move, add, or delete nodes. It can also be used to move the control points in order to modify the slope and shape of the curve. The following Quick Steps demonstrate this.

Shaping a Curve

1. Select the Bézier tool and draw a series of curves similar to Figure 6.4.

2. Select the Shape tool.   The cursor changes into an arrowhead.

3. Select one of the nodes.   The control points appear.

4. Shape the curve by dragging the control points.   The shape and slope of the curve are modified.

5. Drag the selected node to another location.   The segment on either side of the node change shape and slope to accommodate the node's new location.

Figure 6.4

A curve with six nodes.

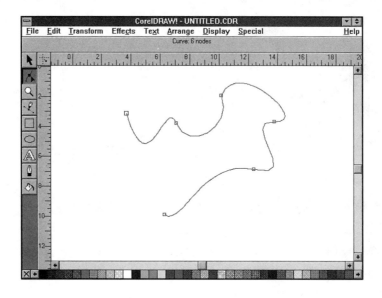

TIP: You can select several nodes by using the Shift-click method or the marquee selection method. The Shift-click method is accomplished by holding down ⇧Shift while selecting each node to be included. With the marquee method, you drag a box around the nodes to select them. When multiple nodes are selected, moving one node will move all selected nodes.

In This Chapter

What Is a Node?

Editing Nodes

Using Fills

Combining Tools and Objects

Changing to and Shaping a Smooth Node

1. Select the Shape tool.
2. Double-click one of the nodes of the curve.
3. Select Smooth from the Node Edit dialog box.

Changing to and Shaping a Symmetrical Node

1. Select the Shape tool.
2. Double-click on a node.
3. Select Symmet from the Node Edit dialog box.

Changing to and Shaping a Cusp Node

1. Select the Shape tool.
2. Double-click on the node.
3. Select Cusp from the Node Edit dialog box.

Adding Nodes

1. Select the Ellipse tool and draw an oval.
2. Select the oval, and press Ctrl+V or select Convert to Curves from the Arrange menu.
3. Select the Shape tool.
4. Double-click between any two of the nodes.
5. Select Add from the Node Edit dialog box.

Changing Multiple Nodes

1. Position the cursor at the upper left corner of the object and drag a selection box around the entire object.
2. Double-click on any one of the nodes.
3. Select Cusp from the Node Edit dialog box.
4. Click the left mouse button inside the work area.

Nodes and Fills

This will be the last chapter devoted to purely basic operations with CorelDRAW!. We still need to know how to edit the various types of nodes, and how to use the fill features. Once we have an understanding of these, we can move on to the really fun stuff—twisting, skewing, and otherwise contorting text. We'll also practice extruding and blending objects and shapes, and use external graphics as a part of our drawings.

What Is a Node?

You already know that a node is found at the point where a line or curve begins, ends, or changes direction. Since nodes are the basis for much of the more sophisticated shaping you will learn later, let's take some time nailing down your understanding of them.

All nodes are not created equal as far as CorelDRAW! is concerned. A node can be a part of either a line or a curve. If it is part of a curve, it can be a *smooth node*, a *symmetrical node*, or a *cusp*. (Don't let this blow you away; the only difference between them is how the control points can be moved.)

Opening the Node Edit Dialog Box

From time to time, you will want to change the characteristics of a node. You may wish, for example, to smooth out or steepen the curve segment on one side of a node, while leaving the other alone. This can be accomplished by using the Node Edit dialog box.

Opening the Node Edit dialog box is a straightforward affair: with the Shape tool selected, double-click on any node of a line or curve. The dialog box shown in Figure 7.1 appears.

Figure 7.1
The Node Edit dialog box.

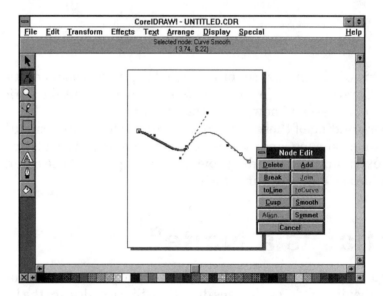

TIP: Nodes "belong to" the line segment or curve that is immediately before them. Selecting a node will also select the preceding line or curve. The segment can then be deleted or broken away by using the Node Edit dialog box's Delete and Break commands.

Changing the Type of Node

The following sets of Quick Steps will illustrate what the different types of nodes are. (The quick steps will assume that you have a curve already drawn. If not, draw one with several nodes that can be changed.)

Smooth Node

A smooth node is distinguished by the fact that its control points are anchored together in a straight line, much like a stick. The major difference is that the distance each control point is from the center can be adjusted, changing the slope of the curve on either side of the node.

Changing to and Shaping a Smooth Node	
1. Select the Shape tool.	The cursor changes to an arrowhead.
2. Double-click one of the nodes of the curve.	Control points and the Node Edit dialog box appear.
3. Select Smooth from the Node Edit dialog box.	The node is changed to a smooth curve node.

To test the smooth node, drag it around in the editing window. Both control points move around the node in an identical fashion, but the slope of the curve associated with each control point can be adjusted individually (see Figure 7.2).

Figure 7.2
In a smooth curve node, the control points will always stay in a straight line.

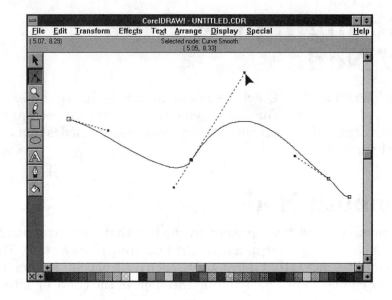

Symmetrical Node

A symmetrical node is the least flexible node. The control points are in a straight line and are at equal distances from the node. The slope on either side of a symmetrical node is identical.

Changing to and Shaping a Symmetrical Node

1. Select the Shape tool.

   Control points appear.

2. Double-click on the node.

   The Node Edit dialog box appears.

3. Select Symmet from the Node Edit dialog box.

   The node is changed to a symmetrical curve node.

To test the symmetrical node, drag it around the editing window. All movements of one control point are mirrored by the other (see Figure 7.3).

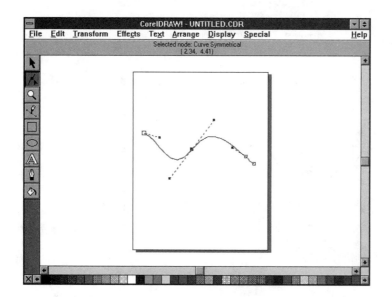

Figure 7.3

Control points of symmetrical curve nodes cannot be separately adjusted— movement of one is mirrored by the other.

Cusp Node

The cusp node is the most flexible of all. It is used whenever radical changes of direction are desired. Each control point can be separately adjusted in direction and distance from the node.

Changing to and Shaping a Cusp Node

1. Select the Shape tool.

   Control points appear.

2. Double-click on the node.

   The Node Edit dialog box appears.

3. Select Cusp from the Node Edit dialog box.

   The node is changed to a cusp curve node.

To test the node, drag it around in the editing window. Each node can be separately adjusted for slope and curve (see Figure 7.4).

Figure 7.4

*Control points on
cusp nodes can
be adjusted
separately.*

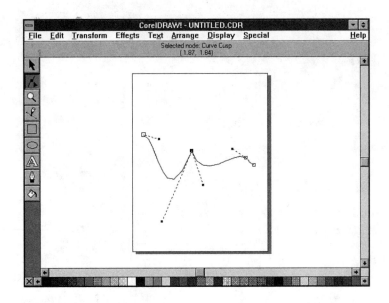

Adding and Deleting Nodes

Nodes can be added to or deleted from any object. Follow these
Quick Steps to add six nodes to an oval.

Adding Nodes

1. Select the Ellipse tool
and draw an oval in
the editing window.

    The oval has one node.

2. Select the oval, and
press Ctrl+V or select
Convert to Curves
from the Arrange
menu.

    The oval becomes a curved
object with four nodes. It
can now be modified with
the Shape tool.

3. Select the Shape tool.

4. Double-click between any two of the nodes on the oval.	The Node Edit dialog box appears.
5. Select Add from the Node Edit dialog box.	A new node is added to the object.
6. Repeat steps 4 and 5 until there are twelve nodes total.	New nodes are added to total twelve (see Figure 7.5).

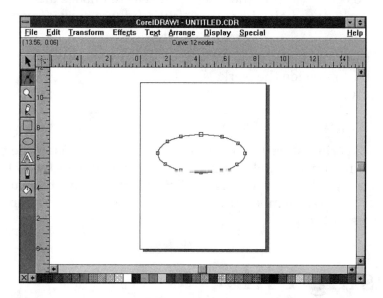

Figure 7.5
A curved object with twelve nodes.

Project 2—Making a Cloud

The oval that we have created can be turned into a cloud with only a little bit of effort. We will first change all of the nodes to cusp nodes (for the maximum flexibility) and reposition them to make the cloud. The following Quick Steps show how to change all the nodes at once.

Changing Multiple Nodes

1. Position the cursor at the upper left corner of the oval and drag a selection box around the entire object.	The status line reads `twelve selected nodes`.
2. Double-click on any one of the nodes.	The Node Edit dialog box appears.
3. Select Cusp from the Node Edit dialog box.	All selected nodes are changed into curved cusp nodes.
4. Click the left mouse button inside the work area.	

Experiment with moving the nodes and modifying the control points until you obtain a shape that would pass for a cloud, something like that in Figure 7.6. Then save your cloud as `proj02.cdr`. (Remember, to save choose Save or Save As from the File menu.)

Using Fills

If an object is composed of a closed path (an area that is completely surrounded by lines) you can fill that area with a variety of colors and patterns. Selecting the Fill tool (the bottom tool in the Toolbox) displays the Fill flyout menu shown in Figure 7.7.

TIP: If you select a fill color with no object selected, that fill will be used as a default.

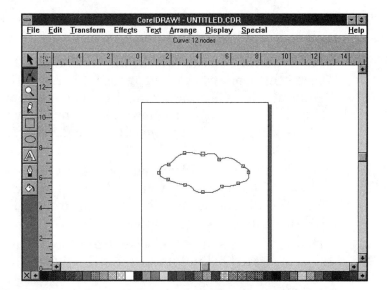

Figure 7.6

Nodes and control points have been modified to obtain a cloud-like shape.

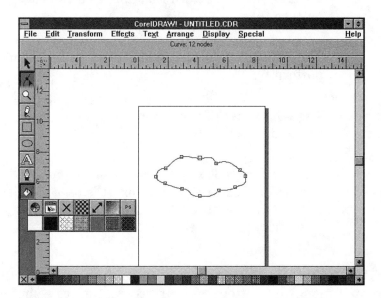

Figure 7.7

The Fill tool's flyout menu.

The following sections show each of the icons from the Fill tool's flyout menu and tell what function each icon performs.

 The Uniform Color icon looks like a color wheel. Using this icon, you can fill any closed area with a uniform color. Clicking on this icon will open up the Uniform Fill dialog box, shown in Figure 7.8, which allows you to select any one of thousands of different colors.

 The Fill Roll-Up window icon opens the Fill Roll-Up window. This will allow you quick access to various fills. The window is very similar to the outline Pen Roll-Up window we have already discussed.

 The None icon makes the object transparent, so objects located behind it can show through.

 The Two-Color Pattern icon applies a two color pattern fill.

 The Full-Color Pattern icon attaches a full color pattern fill.

 The Fountain Fill icon applies fountain fills to selected objects.

 The PostScript Textures icon displays the PostScript Textures dialog box. It is used to select a PostScript texture fill. Unless you have a PostScript printer, this button isn't useful.

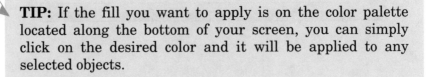

TIP: If the fill you want to apply is on the color palette located along the bottom of your screen, you can simply click on the desired color and it will be applied to any selected objects.

Now that you're familiar with the tools, follow these steps which use a fountain fill to make the cloud into a storm cloud.

1. Select the cloud.

2. Select the Fill tool to open the Fill flyout menu.

3. Select the Fill Roll-Up window icon from the flyout menu. This opens the Fill Roll-Up window shown in Figure 7.9.

4. Select the Fountain Fill icon from the Roll-Up window.

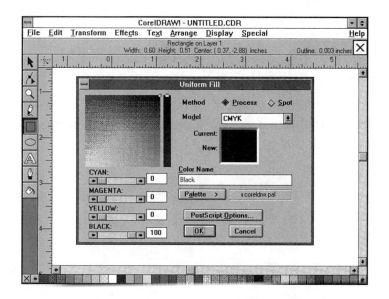

Figure 7.8

The Uniform Fill dialog box.

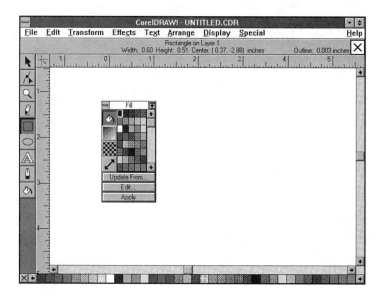

Figure 7.9

The Fill Roll-Up window.

5. Select Edit from the Roll-Up window. The Fountain Fill dialog box will appear.

6. In the Fountain Fill dialog box, select Linear if it's not already selected. The Fountain Fill dialog box will resemble Figure 7.10.

7. Change the Angle to 75.0.

8. Change the From setting to Black.

9. Change the To setting to White.

10. Select OK. The Fountain Fill dialog box closes.

11. Select Apply from the Fill Roll-Up window. The cloud becomes ominous (see Figure 7.11).

Figure 7.10

The Fountain Fill dialog box's Linear options.

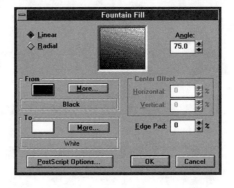

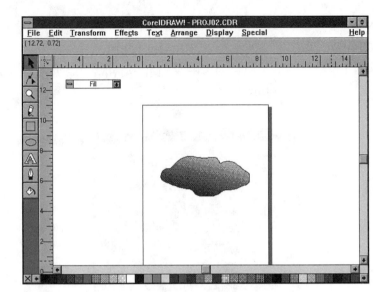

Figure 7.11
The Fountain Fill makes the cloud appear menacing.

What's Next?—Combining Tools and Objects

I hope that you are experimenting with all kinds of different fills. Did you try to change the fill of the cloud to a radial one? Did you change the colors and angles in the Fountain Fill dialog box? In the next chapter you will discover that you can apply these same fills to text.

For now, try this experiment, which reviews what you've learned in this chapter.

1. Draw a circle. (Hold down Ctrl while dragging with the Ellipse tool.)

2. Open the Fill Roll-Up window and select the Fountain Fill icon.

3. Select Edit from the Fill Roll-Up window. This opens the Fountain Fill dialog box.

4. Select Radial. The Fountain Fill dialog box's options change.

5. Change the From setting to Blue (dark blue).

6. Change the To setting to Cyan (light blue).

7. Set both Horizontal and Vertical to 20 degrees. The screen will appear as shown in Figure 7.12

Figure 7.12

The Fountain Fill dialog box's Radial options.

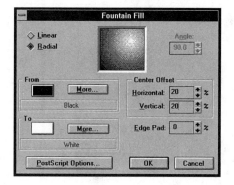

8. Select OK to close the Fountain Fill dialog box.

9. Select Apply from the Fill Roll-Up window to apply the changes to your drawing. The circle takes on a three-dimensional appearance.

10. Make several copies of the filled circle using the Ctrl+D keyboard shortcut.

11. Move two or three of the circles partially on top of the cloud.

12. Select one of them with the Pick tool, and send it to the back of the cloud by selecting To Back from the Arrange menu. The cloud blocks out a part of the circle.

13. Change the thickness of the outline around the circle with the Pen tool.

14. Select another circle, and convert it to curves (as you learned earlier in this chapter).

15. Using the Shape tool and Node Edit dialog box, make the select the circle and click on the yellow swatch of the on-screen color palette.

TIP: How about making one of your circles the sun? Simply select the circle and click on the yellow swatch of the on-screen color palette.

You're done! Your figure might look a little different than mine, shown in Figure 7.13.

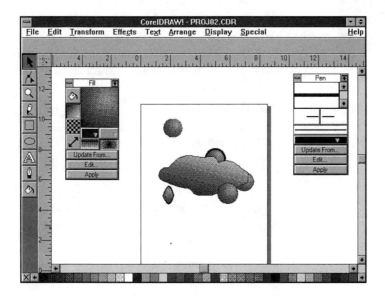

Figure 7.13
The finished drawing. Yours may look a little different.

Congratulations! Not only have you created a rather attractive drawing, you have demonstrated a good grasp of all that you have learned up to this point.

In This Chapter

Adding Text

Importing Text

Editing and Formatting Text

Adding Symbols

Using the Spelling Checker and Thesaurus

Adding Artistic Text

1. Open the Text flyout menu and select A.
2. Move the cursor to where you want to add text, and click the left mouse button.
3. Enter the text.

Adding Paragraph Text

1. Open the Text flyout menu and select A.
2. Move the cursor to where you want to add the text frame.
3. Hold the mouse button down and drag to where you want the frame to end. Then release the mouse button.
4. Type the text.

Using the Text Roll-Up Window

1. Select Text Roll-Up from the Text menu.
2. Select the Text tool.
3. Highlight the words you wish to change.
4. Change font, size, and character attributes in the Text Roll-Up window.
5. Select Apply from the Text Roll-Up window.

Using the Spelling Checker

1. Using the Text or Pick tool, highlight the word or text string to be checked.
2. Select Spelling Checker from the Text menu.
3. Select Check Text and the Always suggest box.
4. Select the proper spelling.

Using the Thesaurus

1. Highlight the word using the Text tool, and select Thesaurus from the Text menu.
2. Select the definition that most closely represents the word as you are using it.
3. Select the appropriate synonym and click on Replace.

Adding and Editing Text

One of CorelDRAW!'s most powerful features is text manipulation. It starts you out with over 150 fonts— even more if you're using the CD-ROM version. Then it gives you the power to bend, rotate, stretch, and otherwise modify the lettering to suit your needs.

About Fonts

Technically, a *font* is a collection of type characters required to set copy in one size and face.

For example, 10-point Times Roman would be one font, while 12-point Times Roman would be another. A typesetter would refer to all of the sizes of type in the Times Roman face as the Times Roman family, while bold and italic would be attributes assigned to individual characters.

In desktop publishing, the introduction of typefaces that can be sized has completely changed how we think about type. True Type Fonts, like those included with CorelDRAW!, Adobe Type Manager's ATM Fonts, and other PostScript compatible fonts, can be scaled "on the fly" to whatever size is wanted. This means that instead of having to purchase an entire family of fonts to have all of the possible sizes, only one is now necessary.

This may sound a bit confusing, but the upshot is that whenever we refer to a font in the desktop publishing field, we are most likely referring to a type family.

NOTE: There is, as you may suspect, a lot of discussion about the merits of each type of font, and which is better for what task. If you want to get involved in the discussion, the Corel Forum in CompuServe is abuzz with folks putting in their thoughts. For our purposes, however, they are all good.

For the exercises in this chapter, you can use any font you like. As you begin working on your own projects, the choice of font will become more important.

Adding Text

Now that you've learned about different fonts, let's look at *why* you use text in CorelDRAW!.

Text is used for two different purposes in CorelDRAW!: decoration and information. CorelDRAW!'s documentation calls decorative text *artistic text*, while informational text is called *paragraph text*. We'll use these terms as well.

The primary difference between the two is the amount of text that will be entered. Artistic text tends to contain only a few letters which are elaborately designed, while paragraph text tends to be longer and less exotic.

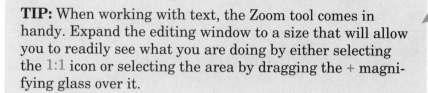

TIP: When working with text, the Zoom tool comes in handy. Expand the editing window to a size that will allow you to readily see what you are doing by either selecting the 1:1 icon or selecting the area by dragging the + magnifying glass over it.

The Text tool is represented in the Toolbox by either the letter A or a star. If you select the Text tool and hold down the mouse button, a flyout menu appears which contains these two icons, so you can choose one or the other (see Figure 8.1). The star is used to add symbols, as you'll learn later. For now, though, you'll be working with regular text, so you'll want to select A.

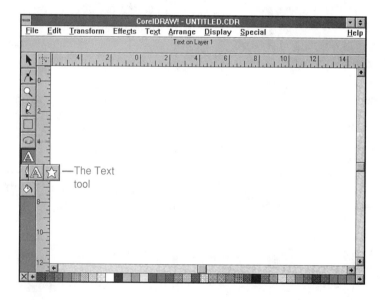

Figure 8.1

The Text tool's flyout menu.

Adding Artistic Text

Artistic text, as was mentioned above, is used for decoration or for special effects. The CorelDRAW! logo is an example of this. You should use artistic text when you will be modifying its appearance by changing individual letters or letter groups.

The following Quick Steps show how to enter artistic text.

Adding Artistic Text

1. Open the Text flyout
   menu by selecting the
   A or star icon and
   holding down the mouse
   button.

2. Select the A from the
   Text flyout menu.

   The cursor changes into a
   cross hair.

3. Move the cursor to the
   location where you
   want to add text, and
   click the left mouse
   button.

   The text position is marked
   by an I-bar.

4. Enter the text.

The positioning of artistic text is not critical. Once the text has been entered, you can select it with the Pick tool and drag it to a new location. As you will see later in this chapter, the free-form nature of artistic text makes manipulating it easy.

Adding Paragraph Text

Paragraph text, because of its length, is added in a frame in CorelDRAW!. The frame is handy, since actions taken on it will affect all of the text it contains. You can size the frame by selecting it and dragging the handles, and you can move the entire frame to another location by dragging it with the mouse.

Adding Paragraph Text

1. Open the Text flyout menu by selecting the A or star icon and holding down the mouse button.

2. Select the A from the Text flyout menu.

   The cursor changes into a cross hair.

3. Move the cursor to the point where you want to add the text frame.

4. Hold the mouse button down and drag it to where you want the frame to end. Then release the mouse button.

   A dotted line surrounds the added frame.

5. Enter the text.

   The text will appear in the editing window.

6. Select the text with the Pick tool.

   A frame surrounds the text. The frame can then be sized and moved.

Adding Text with the Clipboard

As a Windows user, you are probably already familiar with the operation of the clipboard. The clipboard functions as a "common ground" between various Windows applications (and some non-Windows ones). You can Cut or Copy text from an application onto the clipboard, and then Paste the clipboard contents into a different application's drawing or document.

TIP: The shortcut key for the Paste function is `Ctrl`+`Ins`.

The clipboard feature comes in very handy when you want to use text in a graphic file, or vice versa, because you can bypass time-consuming import and export functions. The following Quick Steps explain how to use the clipboard to bring text from a Windows word processor into CorelDRAW!.

Adding Text with the Clipboard

1. Open any Windows word processing program. (Write will work nicely.)

   The word processing program's editing window appears, ready for you to type text.

2. Enter the desired text into the word processor. For our example, enter:

   `I am going to paste this into CorelDRAW!.`

   The text appears on-screen.

3. Highlight the desired text. (To highlight, hold down the left mouse button and drag the pointer.)

   The highlighted text appears in reverse (light letters on a dark background).

4. Select **C**opy from the **E**dit menu, or press `Ctrl`+`C`.

   The text is now on the clipboard.

5. Return to CorelDRAW!. (`Alt`+`Tab↹` will cycle through all open Windows applications.)

   CorelDRAW! becomes active.

6. If you haven't con-
   structed a frame for the
   paragraph text, follow
   steps 1-4 of the Quick
   Steps for Adding
   Paragraph Text.

7. Select **P**aste from the   The text appears in the
   Edit menu, or press   frame.
   Ctrl+Ins.

Importing Text

Importing is one of the few areas where CorelDRAW! stumbles.
Text can only be imported from unformatted ASCII files; text
from word processing programs will not work.

If you need to import text from an external file, it's easiest to
open the file in a Windows-compatible word processor and then
use the cut-and-paste clipboard method just discussed. In most
cases, this will work fine, and is much easier than fooling with
CorelDRAW!'s import feature.

If that won't work, you'll have to attempt an import. Follow
these steps:

1. Construct a paragraph frame, as you learned to do earlier
   in this chapter.

2. Select Import from the **F**ile menu.

3. Select Text, *.TXT for the List Files of Type. If your file
   ends in something other than TXT, change *.TXT to the
   appropriate extension in the File **N**ame box.

4. Specify the file's location in the **D**irectories selection box.
   A list appears of files in that directory which have the
   appropriate extension.

5. Select the file you want, and select OK. Your file *might* be
   imported into CorelDRAW!.

If you are getting the idea that it would be quicker to re-type the information, you are probably right. Remember that CorelDRAW! is a drawing program, not a prepublication layout program like Ventura, Pagemaker, or QuarkXpress.

Editing and Formatting Text

Even though it lacks in some areas of text handling, CorelDRAW! does provide the user with several text editing and formatting tools. Follow these Quick Steps to access the Text dialog box, where text editing takes place.

NOTE: Depending on the type of text selected, the dialog box that appears will be titled either Paragraph Text or Artistic Text. Aside from the name difference, the two dialog boxes look the same. We'll just call it the Text dialog box, for simplicity.

Opening the Text Dialog Box

1. Create (or import) some artistic or paragraph text.

2. Select the text with the Pick tool.

   The text is surrounded with a frame.

3. Select Edit Text from the Edit menu.

   The Text dialog box opens. The one for paragraph text is shown in Figure 8.2.

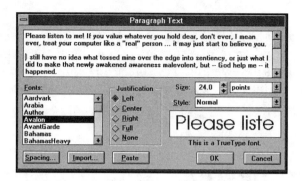

Figure 8.2
*The Paragraph
Text dialog box.*

You can use the various settings in this dialog box to change the attributes (type size, style, justification, and font). For example, if you wanted to change the text to 30-point Avalon, center justified, and bold, you would make the following entries, shown in Figure 8.3.

- Change the Fonts setting to Avalon.

- Select Center as the justification setting.

- Change the Size setting to 30.0 and the unit of measurement to points (if it's not already points).

- Change the Style setting to Bold.

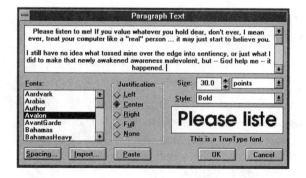

Figure 8.3
*The text attributes
will be changed to
30-point Avalon,
center justified,
and bold.*

Notice that an I-beam cursor appears in the text area at the top of the dialog box. You can make any additions, deletions, or changes to the words themselves here.

> **TIP:** CorelDRAW! looks at text as just another object. This means that you can use the outline tool and the fill tool to modify colors and weight. Try selecting some text and modifying its outline color and weight while assigning a contrasting fill.

Using the Text Roll-Up Window

You may have noticed that changes you make to paragraph text using the dialog box are applied to all of the text in the frame, not just one word or so. You can fine-tune changes to text attributes, and access the tools to change several more, by using the Text Roll-Up window.

The Text Roll-Up window is activated by selecting Text Roll-Up from the Text menu or by pressing Ctrl+2.

Some of the options you can change on the Text Roll-Up window (shown in Figure 8.4) include:

- *Alignment options:* From the top row of buttons on the Text Roll-Up window, you can select left, right, center, full, or no justification.

- *Font:* Just like in the Text dialog box, you can change to any available font.

- *Size:* You can change the size of the letters, and also the unit of measure of the size.

- *Character attributes:* The B button stands for bold, and the I for italic; selecting these buttons will change the character attributes to bold and/or italic. The S with the small S above it represents superscript, and the S with the small S below it stands for subscript.

- *Character kerning:* This option lets you control the spacing between letters.

- *Frame:* Selecting Frame brings up the Frame Attributes dialog box, where you can specify features that you want to apply to the entire frame. This option will be discussed in more detail later in this chapter.

The following Quick Steps show how to open and use this handy window. You will want to experiment with the various options on your own to discover all the ways you can modify your text.

Using the Text Roll-Up Window

1. Select Text Roll-Up from the Text menu.	The Roll-Up window opens.
2. Select the Text tool.	The cursor changes to an I-bar.
3. Highlight the words you wish to change in the editing window.	
4. Change font, size, and character attributes in the Text Roll-Up window.	You will not see the changes until you complete the next step.
5. Select Apply from the Text Roll-Up window.	The changes are made to theselected text (see Figure 8.4).

Changing the Paragraph Text Frame

If you're working with paragraph text, selecting Frame from the Text Roll-Up window will open the Frame Attributes dialog box shown in Figure 8.5. In it, you can choose to have your text displayed in as many as eight columns, and can modify the amount of space between the columns (gutters).

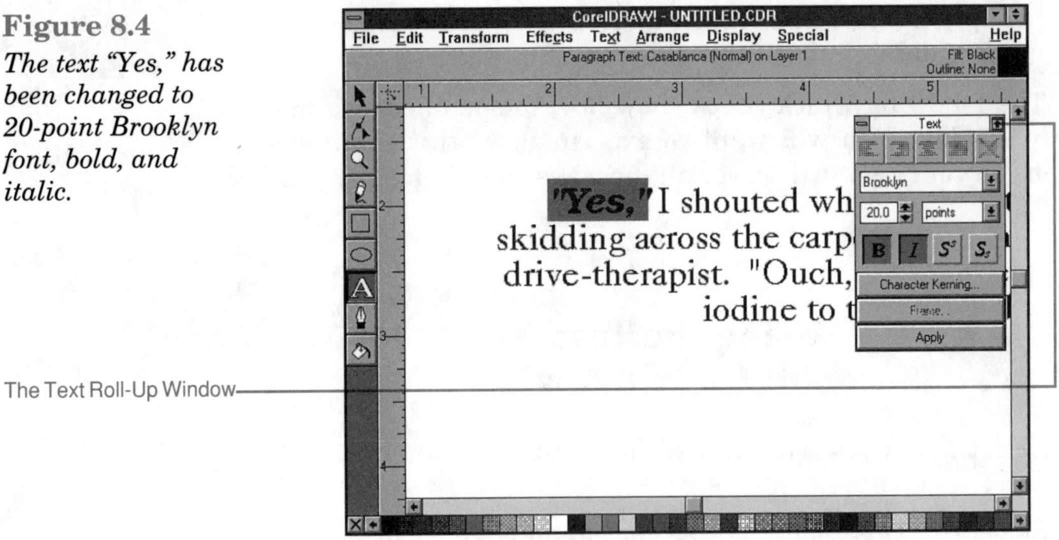

Figure 8.4

The text "Yes," has been changed to 20-point Brooklyn font, bold, and italic.

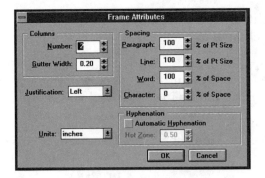

The Text Roll-Up Window

Figure 8.5

The Frame Attributes dialog box.

The Frame Attributes dialog box also allows you to choose to have the text hyphenated by CorelDRAW!. The *Hot Zone* measurement determines the area within which words can be hyphenated. The Hot Zone is a rather advanced concept; you may want to read more about it in your CorelDRAW! manual. The same goes for the Spacing options available here.

Advanced modifications of this kind are usually done in page layout programs, but it's sometimes quite useful to have access to these tools for that one-page flyer, or simple advertising piece. For example, Figure 8.6 shows text formatted with the information shown in Figure 8.5, two columns left-justified with a 0.20 gutter.

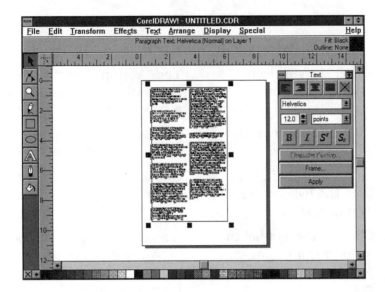

Figure 8.6
The Paragraph Frame has been reformatted into two columns with a 0.20" gutter.

Adding Symbols

CorelDRAW! comes with numerous symbols that can be quickly and easily added into any of your drawings. If you did a full installation of CorelDRAW!, the symbols were installed automatically. (If not, you may want to go back and install a few of them to use with this exercise.)

One of my favorite symbols that comes with CorelDRAW! is a penguin. Follow along with these Quick Steps as we place a three-inch high penguin in the editing window. (You can use any symbol you like.)

Adding a Symbol

1. Hold down the mouse button on the Text tool until the Text flyout menu appears.

continues

Adding a Symbol *continued*

2. Select the star icon.

The "A" icon changes to a star and the cursor becomes a cross hair.

3. Click anywhere in the editing window.

The Symbols Dialog box appears (see Figure 8.7).

4. Select a symbol group from the list (for our example, select Animals).

One of the symbols in the set appears.

5. Click on the symbol that appears (for our example, it's a picture of a man).

A scroll box appears showing all of the symbols in that group. (For our example, it's 100 animal symbols.)

6. Select the symbol you want (for example, the penguin). Or, if you know the symbol number, enter it in the Symbol #: box.

The selected symbol is shown.

7. Change the setting in the Size box as desired. For our example, set it to 3.00 inches.

8. Select OK.

The symbol appears in the editing window (a three-inch penguin, if you followed the example).

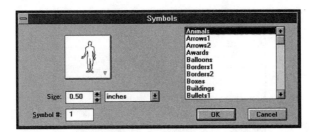

Figure 8.7
*The Symbols
dialog box.*

What's Next?—Using the Spelling Checker and Thesaurus

Using CorelDRAW!'s built-in Spelling Checker and Thesaurus is an easy task. Follow along with these Quick Steps as we check suspicious spelling.

Using the Spelling Checker

1. Using the Text or Pick tool, highlight the word or text string to be checked.

2. Select Spell Checker from the Text menu.

   The Spelling Checker dialog box opens, as shown in Figure 8.8.

3. Select Check Text and the Always suggest box.

   A list of alternative words appears.

4. Select the proper spelling.

   The word is corrected.

If an entire text string had been selected, the Spelling Checker would only stop on words that it did not recognize.

Figure 8.8
*The Spelling
Checker dialog
box.*

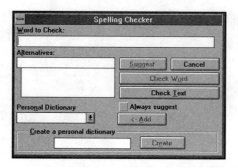

Most documents contain at least a few words that are not recognized by the Spelling Checker, like trademark names or industry-specific terms. You can add these terms to a customized dictionary. With the Spelling Checker dialog box open, follow these steps:

1. Enter a name in the Create a personal dictionary field.

2. When the Spelling Checker finds a word that it doesn't recognize, select Add to add it to the dictionary.

CorelDRAW! also comes with a thesaurus for looking up synonyms. Use of the Thesaurus is, if anything, even easier than using the Spelling Checker. Here are the Quick Steps that show how:

Using the Thesaurus

1. Highlight the word using the Text tool, and select Thesaurus from the Text menu.

The Thesaurus dialog box opens and suggests definitions and synonyms for the word selected, as shown in Figure 8.9.

2. Select the definition that most closely represents the word as you are using it.

3. Select the appropriate
synonym and click on
Replace.

The synonym is substituted
for the initial word.

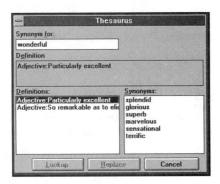

Figure 8.9
*The Thesaurus
dialog box suggests
alternatives for the
word "wonderful."*

In This Chapter

Adjusting Text Spacing

Copying Text Attributes

Fitting Text to a Path

Opening the Text Spacing Dialog Box

1. Select the text with the Pick tool.
2. Select Edit Text from the Edit menu.
3. Select Spacing.

Copying Text Attributes

1. Use the Pick tool to select the text string that you want to change.
2. Select Copy Style From from the Edit menu.
3. Select what you want to copy, and select OK.
4. Select the text string from which you wish to copy the attributes.

Adjusting Text Orientation

1. Select both the text and the path it is to follow.
2. Open the Fit Text To Path Roll-Up window (Ctrl+F).
3. Select the arrow next to the capital letters.
4. Select the desired text orientation.
5. Select Apply.

Advanced Text Manipulation

Since CorelDRAW! is designed to create and modify the appearance of objects, it should come as no surprise that there are many ways to modify the appearance of text. This chapter will introduce you to some of these methods, including text spacing, text orientation, and text mirroring. You will also learn how to fit text to a path, one of CorelDRAW!'s neatest features.

Adjusting Text Spacing

In a word processing program, you are often limited to standard text spacing—you can choose how many spaces you want between words, letters, and lines, but you cannot change the size of the individual spaces. Not so with CorelDRAW!. One of its most useful features is the ability to adjust the spacing between characters, words, lines, and paragraphs.

The following Quick Steps show how to open the Text Spacing dialog box, from which you can perform these adjustments.

Opening the Text Spacing Dialog Box

1.	Select the text with the Pick tool.	Text is surrounded with a frame.
2.	Select Edit Text from the Edit menu.	The Artistic or Paragraph Text dialog box opens, depending on the type of text selected.
3.	Select Spacing.	The Text Spacing dialog box opens (see Figure 9.1).

Figure 9.1
The Text Spacing dialog box.

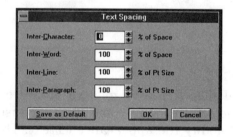

Changing any of the measurements in the Text Spacing dialog box will change the spacing in all of the text that has been selected. Percentage measurements are used since the space represented by the percentage will increase or decrease as the type is scaled. Here's a list of the settings and what they're used for.

The *Inter-Character* measurement is used to increase or decrease the space between characters. Positive numbers will increase the space between characters; negative numbers will decrease it.

The *Inter-Word* measurement operates the same way as the Inter-Character measurement, except that modifications apply to the space between words.

Inter-Line spacing, also known as leading, is adjusted in increments of point size. Numbers above 100% will increase the space between lines; numbers below 100% will decrease it.

Inter-Paragraph spacing works the same way as Inter-Line spacing, except that it applies the spacing to hard paragraph returns.

Advanced Spacing Options

Even finer adjustments to spacing can be made in *interactive* mode. If you select text with the Shape tool, you will see a box similar to the one in Figure 9.2 surrounding the text.

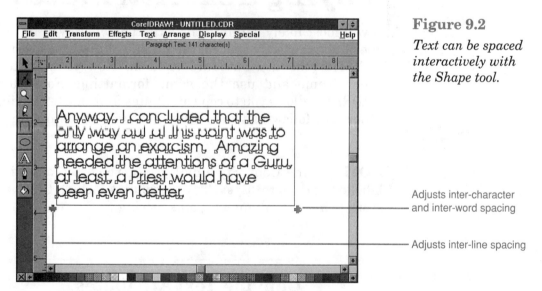

Figure 9.2

Text can be spaced interactively with the Shape tool.

Adjusts inter-character and inter-word spacing

Adjusts inter-line spacing

The icon in the bottom right corner of the frame is used to adjust inter-character and inter-word spacing. Dragging this icon to the right will increase the spacing between letters, and dragging it to the left will decrease the spacing. Dragging the icon while pressing Ctrl will change the inter-word spacing.

Inter-line spacing is adjusted by dragging the icon in the lower left corner up (to decrease the leading) or down (to increase it).

TIP: You can also reposition any one of the letters by selecting the box at the letter's lower left corner and dragging it around. This same procedure, selecting an individual letter, is useful if you want to change the fill or outline characteristics of that letter only.

Copying Text Attributes

You will most likely run into the situation where you have one frame of text perfectly spaced, the fill and outline are just right, and all of its other attributes are "right on." Now, you want to add another frame and use the same formatting. Fortunately, CorelDRAW! allows you to copy attributes from one text string to another. The following Quick Steps illustrate this procedure.

NOTE: In the Copy Style dialog box, you'll see a setting labelled text attributes. Text attributes include typeface, style, point size, alignment, and spacing.

Copying Text Attributes

1. Use the Pick tool to select the text string that you want to change.

2. Select Copy Style From from the Edit menu.   The Copy Style dialog box appears (see Figure 9.3).

3. Select what you want to copy, and select OK.

You are returned to the drawing and the cursor has changed to a FROM? arrow (see Figure 9.4).

4. Select the string that you wish to copy the attributes from.

The cursor changes back to that of the Pick tool, and the attributes are copied.

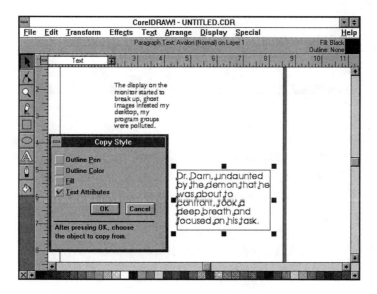

Figure 9.3
The Copy Style dialog box.

Fitting Text to a Path

TIP: Throughout the rest of this book, you will be learning techniques that will give even the most well-equipped computer a real workout. If you find that you are having to wait a very long time for the screen to redraw, try toggling into Wireframe mode by pressing ⏷Shift+F9. This will paint only the outlines of your work on the screen, but will still save everything. You can view the complete drawing at any time by pressing ⏷Shift+F9 again.

Figure 9.4

*Point the FROM?
cursor at the text
string containing
the desired
attributes.*

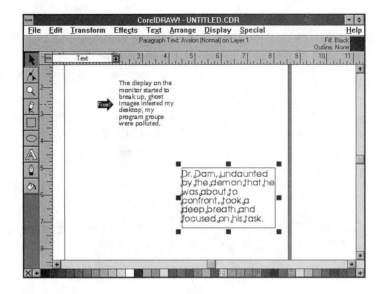

In most programs, text must run in a straight line—usually horizontally across the page. While easy to read, text in a straight line can be boring and plain.

To combat this kind of boredom, CorelDRAW! allows you to fit text to a path. Simply put, this means that you can create a shape and then make the text wrap around it. Fitting text can be a lot of fun—don't forget to sleep and eat once you've started playing with it!

Creating The Apple Corps Logo

Perhaps the best way to get you excited about fitting text is to show you how it's done. So follow the steps to create a new logo for that grade-school-aged, counter-insurgency and espionage group, the dreaded Apple Corps.

1. Click and hold on the Text icon until the Text flyout menu opens.

2. Select the star icon from the Text flyout menu.

3. Click in the editing window to open the Symbol dialog box.

4. Select Food from the list of symbol types.

5. Select the first symbol, the apple core, and set its Size to 2 inches. Your editing window should look like Figure 9.5.

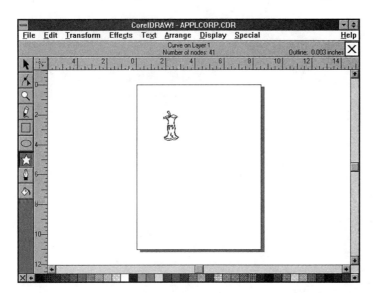

Figure 9.5

The apple core symbol.

6. Select the Ellipse tool, and while holding down Ctrl, draw a circle approximately 2.5 inches in height anywhere in the editing window.

TIP: Remember that Ctrl will constrain an ellipse to a circle, and the height of the circle will be displayed in the status bar.

7. Select the circle and drag it over the apple core.

8. Click and hold on the Text tool again until the Text flyout menu reappears, and select the A.

9. Type The Apple Corps anywhere in the editing window.

10. Select the text with the Pick tool, and either using the Text Roll-Up window, Ctrl+2, or the Character command

in the Text menu, change the typeface into something appropriate, like 36-point Frankenstein.

11. Select both the text and the circle by holding down ⇧Shift and clicking on each item. Your screen should now look like Figure 9.6.

Figure 9.6

The circle and text are selected.

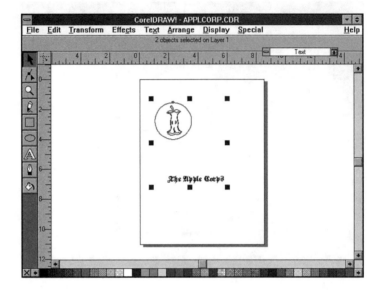

12. Select Fit Text to Path from the Text menu. The Fit Text To Path Roll-Up window opens, as shown in Figure 9.7.

13. Select Apply. After a short wait, the text fits itself to the circle.

14. Make the circle "disappear" by selecting it and choosing the X icon from the Outline tool's flyout menu.

Your drawing will now look like Figure 9.8. It is now suitable for silk screening on the jacket of each and every "terrorist" in Public School 22.

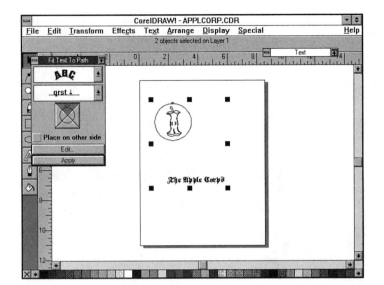

Figure 9.7

The Fit Text To Path Roll-Up window.

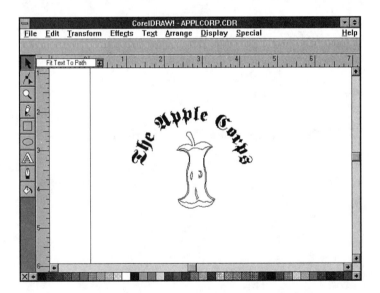

Figure 9.8

The Apple Corps logo.

Controlling How Letters Sit on a Path

You may have noticed that in our logo the letters "sat" on the path of the curve. In other words, the top and the bottom of each letter followed the path of the curve. CorelDRAW! allows you to adjust this in four different manners (see Figure 9.9):

- Rotated Letters
- Vertical Skew
- Horizontal Skew
- Upright Letters

Figure 9.9

The four different text orientations.

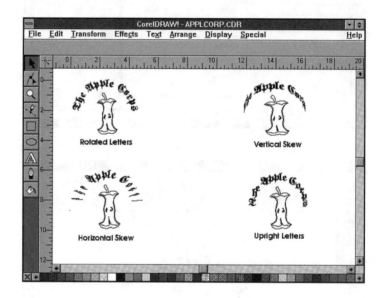

The following Quick Steps show how to change the text orientation.

Adjusting Text Orientation

1. Select both the text and the path it is to follow.

   A box surrounds both objects.

2. Open the Fit Text To Path Roll-Up window (Ctrl+F).

   The Roll-Up window appears in the editing window.

3. Select the arrow next to the capital letters.

A drop-down menu opens, as shown in Figure 9.10.

4. Select the desired text orientation.

5. Select Apply.

The orientation of the selected text is changed.

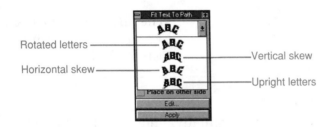

Rotated letters
Horizontal skew
Vertical skew
Upright letters

Figure 9.10

The text orientation drop-down menu.

Designating the Distance from the Path

In all of the work you have done so far, the text has sat directly on the designated path. There will be times, however, when you want text to be above or below the path. That's OK—CorelDRAW! can handle it. The following Quick Steps show how you can reposition the text above, below, or even in the middle of the path line.

Changing Distance from the Path

1. Select the text.

2. Press Ctrl+F to open the Fit Text To Path Roll-Up window.

continues

Changing Distance from the Path *continued*

3. Select the arrow next to the lowercase letters on the Roll-Up window.

A drop-down menu opens, as shown in Figure 9.11.

4. Select the desired alignment option (see Figure 9.11).

5. Select Apply.

The distance of the text string from the path is established.

The last option—manually adjusting the distance—is also quite easy to use. Once this option has been selected, you can click and drag the text any distance that you may want from the path. The text will position itself at the selected distance, while still following the path.

Figure 9.11

Options from this drop-down menu establish the text's relation to the path.

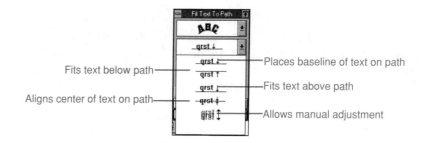

Fits text below path
Aligns center of text on path
Places baseline of text on path
Fits text above path
Allows manual adjustment

Adjusting Path Alignment

When you are fitting text to an ellipse or rectangle, the Fit Text To Path Roll-Up window will contain the icon of a square and circle divided into four parts (refer to Figure 9.7). Each part of this circle represents one of the quadrants of the ellipse or rectangle to which you want to fit text.

To align your text, select the proper quadrant on the menu. The center point of your text string will then align with the center point of the selected quadrant.

If the path is not an ellipse or rectangle, you will see a third option on the Fit Text To Path menu. The option is represented by the letters "abc" with an arrow pointing in from the right. When selected, a drop-down menu appears (see Figure 9.12). The three choices represent aligning text left, center, and right on the selected path.

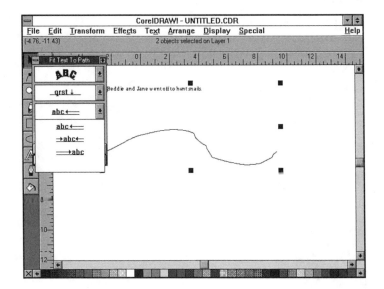

Figure 9.12

The choices represent aligning text left, center, and right on the selected path.

After you have selected the justification, the drop-down menu will close and you will see a box labeled Place on other side (see Figure 9.13). Checking this box will mirror the text on the opposite side of the path, turning it upside down and backwards.

QUICK STEPS

Mirroring Text on a Path

1. Select the text and its path.

2. Press Ctrl+F to open the Fit Text To Path Roll-Up window.

3. Select the desired alignment option.

4. Select Place on Other Side.

5. Select Apply.   The selected text is mirrored.

Figure 9.13

The Fit Text To Path drop-down menu.

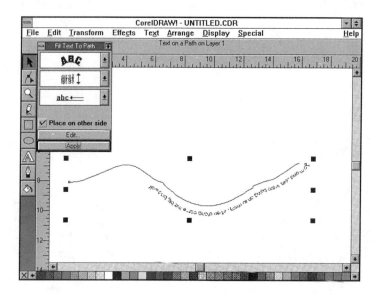

If you want to maintain the same starting point, choose the opposite justification.

You now know enough of the basics of CorelDRAW! to construct a multitude of projects. There will be times, however, when you really want to become fancy, and the rest of this book is devoted to teaching you how to do just that. Chapters 10 and 11 will introduce you to some of the special effects that you can apply to your art. Chapter 12 will give you instructions on using color.

In This Chapter

Adding Perspective

Copying Perspective

Shaping with Envelopes

Copying Envelopes

Adding Perspective

1. Select the group of objects with the Pick tool.
2. Select Edit Perspective from the Effects menu.
3. Place the cursor over one of the handles on the upper portion of the page.
4. Hold down Ctrl and ⬆Shift while you drag the handle toward the center of the tracks.
5. Release the mouse button.

Changing Perspective with the Vanishing Point

1. Select the drawing with the Shape tool.
2. Use the vertical scroll bar to scroll the drawing until the vanishing point icon appears.
3. Place the cursor on the vanishing point.
4. Relocate the vanishing point anywhere you wish.

Copying Perspective

1. Use the Pick tool to select the object or text that you want to format with an existing perspective.
2. Select Copy Perspective From from the Effects menu.
3. Select the object from which you wish to copy the perspective.

Applying an Envelope

1. Use the Pick tool to select the object or group of objects that you wish to reshape.
2. Select Edit Envelope from the Effects menu.
3. Select one of the four editing modes.
4. Use the cursor to drag the handles in the desired direction(s).

Chapter

10

Special Effects, Part I

The last chapters in this book deal with special effects. This material is quite advanced, so don't be alarmed if it takes a while to understand. Additionally, this can really make your computer work. The information on perspective should be quite easy to grasp, as will the basics of envelopes.

Perspective

In the real world, things don't appear flat. Objects that are far away appear small, while those that are close appear large. Perhaps the most familiar way to think of perspective is to imagine railroad tracks disappearing into the distance. This illusion of depth is easily accomplished with CorelDRAW!.

Adding Perspective

Figure 10.1 is a simple picture of a set of railroad tracks. It is composed of straight lines and it has been grouped. If you want to follow along with the example in this section, go ahead and create a similar figure on your screen. (If you've gotten this far in the book, creating a simple drawing like this one should be easy!)

Figure 10.1

A simple railroad track drawing.

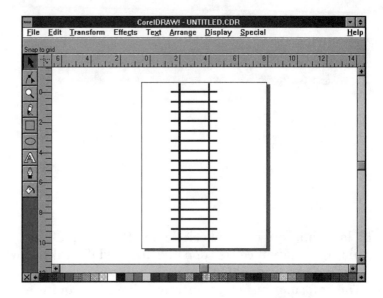

Ready? Good. Now follow these Quick Steps to add perspective to the drawing.

Adding Perspective

1. Select the group of objects with the Pick tool.	The status line will read `Group of x objects on layer one` (*x* will be a number).

2. Select Edit Perspective from the Effects menu. If the Edit Perspective selection is grayed out, check to be sure that you have grouped the objects.

A dashed box with four small handles appears around the selected objects, and the cursor changes to an arrowhead.

3. Place the cursor over one of the handles on the upper portion of the page.

The cursor shape changes to a cross hair.

4. Hold down Ctrl and ⇧Shift while you drag the handle towards the center of the tracks.

Ctrl constrains movement, while ⇧Shift moves the opposite handle at the same time. (You can modify each handle individually by not holding down ⇧Shift.)

5. Release the mouse button.

Perspective is applied to the drawing (see Figure 10.2).

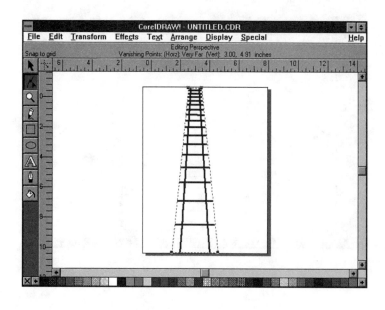

Figure 10.2
Perspective has been added to the tracks.

If at any time you don't like what you have done, simply select Clear Perspective from the Effects menu, and all changes to the perspective of the selected object will be cleared.

> **TIP:** Although we have only talked about changing the perspective on the vertical axis (by moving the upper, or lower, two handles toward or away from each other), you can modify the horizontal perspective by moving an upper and lower handle toward or away from each other.

Altering Perspective

If perspective has been applied to an object, anytime you select that object with the Shape tool, a new icon will appear. If you scroll your drawing up a little bit, you will see an X icon, like that shown in Figure 10.3. This icon is called the *vanishing point*, and it can be manipulated, too. Follow these Quick Steps to learn how.

Figure 10.3
The vanishing point.

Vanishing point ——————

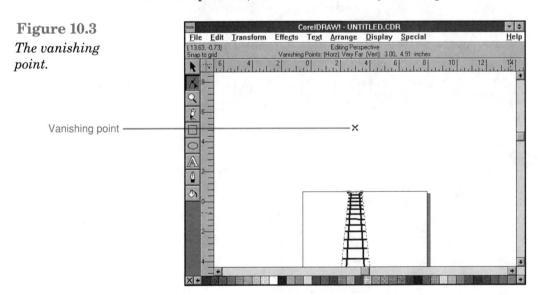

Changing Perspective with the Vanishing Point

1. Select the railroad tracks with the Shape tool.	A dashed box appears, and the cursor changes to an arrowhead.
2. Use the vertical scroll bar to scroll the drawing until the vanishing point icon appears.	
3. Place the cursor on the vanishing point.	The cursor changes to a cross hair.
4. Relocate the vanishing point anywhere you wish.	The entire object will change to conform to the location of the vanishing point.

TIP: Moving the point closer to the drawing increases the perspective effect; moving it further away decreases the effect.

Multiple-Point Perspective

Thus far, we have learned how to change the perspective either on the horizontal or on the vertical axis. In the real world, however, perspective is not limited to only one dimension.

The application of two-point perspective is quite simple. With one vanishing point appearing, say on the vertical axis like the railroad track, apply horizontal perspective by dragging one of the upper handles towards the bottom.

Figure 10.4 shows the railroad track with two-point perspective. It looks as if it is starting to wrap around itself.

Figure 10.4

Two-point perspective has been applied to the railroad tracks. The drawing now has two vanishing points.

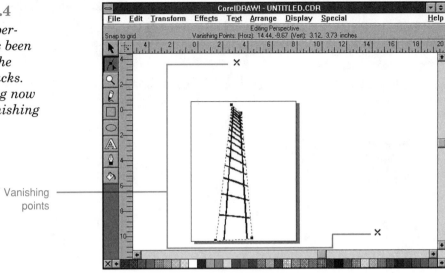

Vanishing points

Copying Perspective

You will often want to copy the perspective of one object to another. This helps to maintain the professional appearance of your work by keeping the vanishing points in line.

Figure 10.5 shows a cover sheet with the words "CorelDRAW!" and "Perspective" in 70-point bold Avalon typeface. Perspective has been added to "CorelDRAW!" by modifying the handles (pulling the left ones apart and pushing the right ones together). If you want to try copying perspective, as shown in the following Quick Steps, go ahead and type in these two words and set up the perspective shown.

QUICK STEPS

Copying Perspective

1. Use the Pick tool to select the object or text that you want to format with an existing perspective.

2. Select Copy Perspective From from the Effects menu.

The cursor changes to the From? arrow (see Figure 10.6).

3. Select the object that you wish to copy the perspective *from*.

The perspective is copied to the new object, as shown in Figure 10.7.

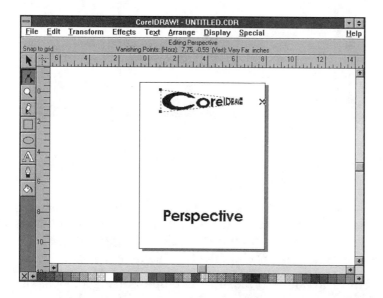

Figure 10.5
Preparing to copy perspective from the text at the top of the screen.

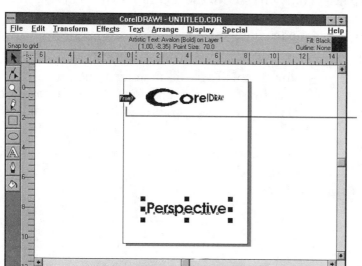

Figure 10.6
The cursor changes to the FROM? arrow.

The From? arrow

Figure 10.7

Perspective has been copied.

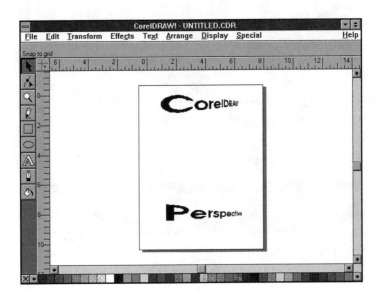

Shaping with Envelopes

Imagine that your art has been printed on the surface of a balloon. You can take that balloon and stretch it in a number of ways, and each stretch distorts your art work. CorelDRAW! mimics this distortion with the special effect called an *envelope*.

There are four different envelope editing modes, three of which affect only one side of the object. As we shall see, the fourth allows some rather dramatic text-fitting. The tools you use to apply these modes include:

 The Straight Line tool stretches the envelope in one direction. (Think of placing a rubber band around two fingers and stretching it with your other hand. The fingers act like anchors, and the rubber band stretches in straight lines away from them.)

 The Single Arc tool is used to stretch the envelope into a simple curve, much like a string loosely draped over two fingers.

The Two Curves tool is used to stretch the envelope into a complex curve, similar to the letter S.

 The Unconstrained tool—as its name suggests—is used to obtain some pretty wild shapes.

Follow these Quick Steps to learn how to apply an envelope.

Applying an Envelope

1. Use the Pick tool to select the object or group of objects that you wish to reshape.

2. Select Edit Envelope from the Effects menu. — A flyout menu appears (see Figure 10.8).

3. Select one of the four editing modes. — The Shape tool is selected and the object is surrounded by a box with eight handles.

4. Use the cursor to drag the handles in the desired direction(s). — The envelope is distorted.

Figures 10.9, 10.10, and 10.11 demonstrate the results that can be obtained by the first three modes.

The Unconstrained envelope editing mode is the most flexible of all. It allows you to select and move multiple nodes at the same time, just like you could when shaping lines. It also gives you access to control points, again just like using the Shape tool on a node.

Figure 10.8
The Editing Mode menu.

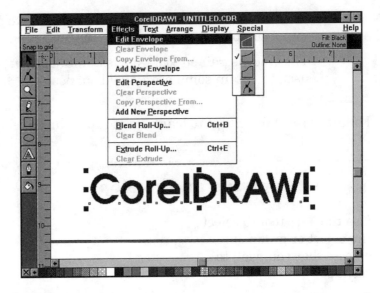

Figure 10.9
The Straight Line Editing Mode.

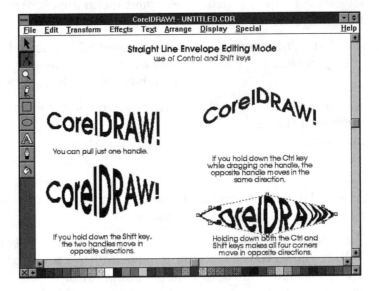

The only way to learn how to use the unconstrained envelope editing mode is to use it. With sufficient practice, you will be able to apply this envelope to drawings to obtain some really awesome effects.

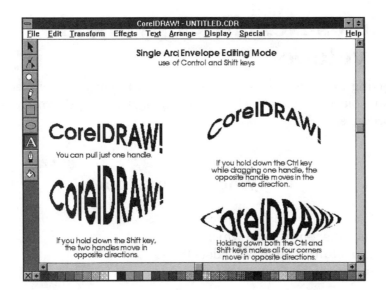

Figure 10.10
The Single Arc Envelope Editing Mode.

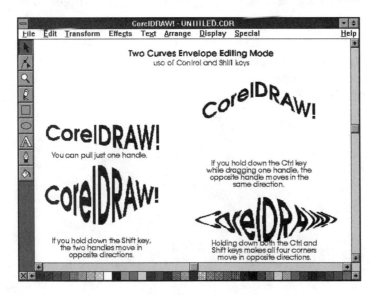

Figure 10.11
The Two Curves Envelope Editing Mode.

What's Next?—Copying an Envelope

Copying an envelope is almost identical to copying perspective from object to object. The following Quick Steps explain the procedure.

Copying an Envelope	
1. Use the Pick tool to select the object or text to which you want to apply an existing envelope format.	
2. Select Copy Envelope From from the Effects menu.	The cursor changes to the From? arrow.
3. Click on the object that you wish to copy the envelope *from*.	The envelope is copied.

In This Chapter

A Simple Extrusion

*Changing Perspective
and Depth*

*Altering Spatial
Orientation*

Creating Shading Effects

Coloring the Extrusion

*Seeing How It All Works
Together*

Blending Objects

Extruding

1. Enter the text or create the object that you wish to extrude.

2. Use the Pick tool to select the text, and apply any other effects if you wish.

3. Press Ctrl+E to open the Extrude Roll-Up window.

4. Select Apply from the Extrude Roll-Up window.

5. Select the Outline tool.

Rotating a Perspective Extrusion

1. Select the desired object.

2. Open the Extrude Roll-Up window.

3. Make sure the Perspective box is selected.

4. Select the 3-D rotation icon.

5. Select the Edit box (if it is not grayed out).

6. Click on any of the six arrows to rotate the object to the position desired.

7. Select Apply.

Blending

1. If necessary, create the first object of the blend.

2. Create the second object of the blend.

3. Select both objects (Press ⇧Shift and click on both).

4. Press Ctrl+B to open the Blend Roll-Up window.

5. Select 10 steps and a 45 degree rotation, and select Apply.

Special Effects, Part II

Well, you've come a long way in this book since drawing your first lines. You've learned about shapes, curves, colors, outlines, and many other drawing techniques. In this chapter, you'll be combining many of the effects you've learned about, plus learning a few more tricks.

A great way to think of an extrusion is to imagine a cookie dough gun. You can put, for example, a star template in the cookie gun, press the trigger, and out comes a star that can be as deep as you want it to be. In the same manner, extrusions apply depth to text or other objects.

Follow these Quick Steps to see a simple extrusion in action.

TIP: Extrusions can take a very long time to draw on your computer screen. Unless you have an extremely expensive video card, and even if you do, you can save a lot of time by using wireframe mode, ⌈⇧Shift⌉+⌈F9⌉, for everything but viewing the final fruits of your labor.

Extruding

1. Enter the text or create the object that you wish to extrude. In the figure, I have entered SPECIAL EFFECTS in 30-point bold Avalon typeface.

2. Use the Pick tool to select the text, and apply any other effects if you wish. I have applied a Single Arc Envelope to obtain the shape shown in Figure 11.1.

   Figure 11.1 shows the figure zoomed at 1:1.

3. Press Ctrl+E to open the Extrude Roll-Up window.

   Your screen will look something like Figure 11.2.

4. Select Apply from the Extrude Roll-Up window.

   When your screen redraws, it will appear to be a black blob.

5. Select the Outline tool and choose white (or any light color).

   You have created your first extrusion (see Figure 11.3).

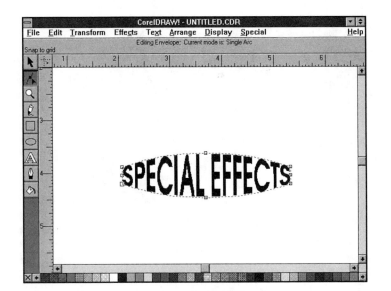

Figure 11.1
Text has been modified with a Single Arc envelope.

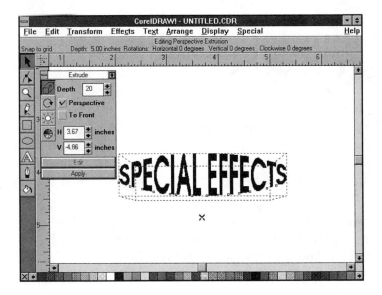

Figure 11.2
The Extrude Roll-Up window is opened. (Note the presence of a vanishing point.)

Figure 11.3
A white outline pen is applied to complete the extrude.

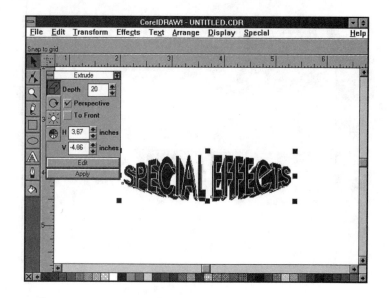

Changing Perspective and Depth

Let's look closer now at the Extrude Roll-Up window that you saw in Figure 11.2. The Depth icon is used to set the location of an extrusion's vanishing point, depth, and direction. It is also used to set whether or not the extrusion will have perspective. The following Quick Steps will show you how to establish a vanishing point for extrusion.

The vanishing point of an extrusion is identical to the vanishing point we learned about in Chapter 10, with the exception that it applies to a more complex object.

Establishing a Vanishing Point

QUICK STEPS

1. Enter the text or create the object that you wish to extrude. I selected the text from the previous exercise and invoked the Clear Extrude command from the Effects menu.

2. Press Ctrl+E to open the Extrude Roll-Up window.

3. Position the cursor on the vanishing point (the X icon) and drag it to a new location.

   If the Perspective box on the Extrude Roll-Up window is checked, the dashed outline box changes to reflect the new vanishing point. If not, the "back" of the object is moved to the location of the icon.

4. Select Apply.

   The new vanishing point is applied to the object.

The horizontal and vertical measurements on the Extrude Roll-Up window tell you the location of the vanishing point with relation to the zero point on the rulers. Therefore, you can relocate the zero points to obtain accurate measurements of the object, or by inputting your own numbers, you can accurately establish the size of the extrusion.

If the perspective box is checked, the depth counter sets the extent of the extrusion. If the counter is set to the maximum number, 99, the extrusion will extend all of the way to the vanishing point. As this number grows smaller, the extrusion will recede from the vanishing point, becoming shallower while maintaining the selected perspective.

Rotating a Perspective Extrusion

The 3-D Rotation icon on the Extrude Roll-Up window (the second one from the top) allows you to alter the orientation of the object, rotating it through three dimensions. When you select this icon, the extrude rotator appears (see Figure 11.4). If the perspective box was selected, the entire object can be rotated. If the box was not checked, only the face of the extrusion will be rotated.

Figure 11.4

The Extrude Rotator allows you to rotate an extrusion.

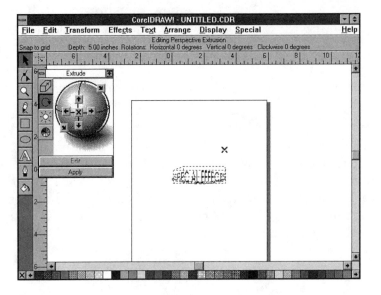

The following Quick Steps summarize the procedure for rotating an object.

Rotating a Perspective Extrusion

1. Select the desired object.

A bounding box surrounds the selected object.

2. Open the Extrude Roll-Up window.

3. Make sure the Perspective box is selected.

4. Select the 3-D rotation icon.

A dashed bounding box surrounds the object and the vanishing point is visible.

5. If the Edit box is not grayed out, select it.

If the Edit box is grayed out, it is already selected.

6. Click on any of the six arrows to rotate the object to the position desired.

A dashed bounding box will rotate around the extrusion.

7. Select Apply.

The object is rotated.

The procedure for modifying the orientation of an object without perspective (this kind of object is called *orthogonal*) is similar, except that only the extruded face moves.

Creating Shading Effects

The third icon on the Extrude Roll-Up window, the Light Source Direction icon, lets you simulate a light source hitting the object and casting shadows. When you select the Light Source Direction icon, you will see the options shown in Figure 11.5.

Figure 11.5

*Selecting the Light
Source Direction
icon displays new
options in the
Extrude Roll-Up
window.*

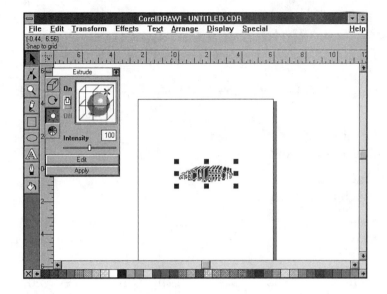

The first thing you may notice is the light switch. Clicking on this switch turns the light source on and off. Immediately to the right of the switch is a wireframe cube, representing the location of the light source. The sphere represents the extruded object.

You can move the light source by clicking on the wireframe where two lines meet.

The intensity of the light source is controlled by the field at the bottom right of the box. The value 100 is the default. As the numbers decrease towards zero, the intensity of the light fades to black. Numbers approaching 200 make the brilliance approach white.

Coloring the Extrusion

The fourth icon is called the Extrusion Coloring icon. Using this icon allows you to apply different colors to the surfaces that are extruded from an object. Figure 11.6 shows the three options available:

- *Use Object Fill* will color the extruded surfaces with the same color that is used for the fill of the original object.

- *Solid Fill* allows you to choose any solid color to all extruded surfaces.

- *Shade* allows you to create the effect of one color blending into another along the extruded surfaces.

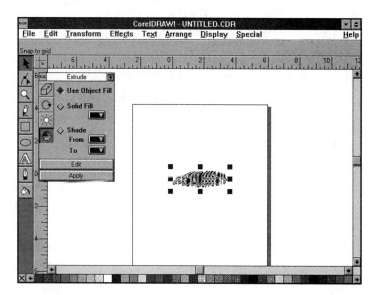

Figure 11.6

Available extrusion coloring options.

Seeing How It All Works Together

Whew! You've learned a lot of complicated stuff in this chapter! Now follow these steps to see how it all works together.

1. Select New from the File menu. Save your current work under a new name if you wish.

2. Type EXTRUDE in any 30-point bold typeface.

3. Zoom as necessary and apply a Two Curves envelope.

4. Select the text and click on the light gray color swatch on the bottom of the screen. The fill of the text becomes light gray.

5. Select the Outline pen tool and click on the solid black box in the flyout menu. The text is outlined in black.

6. Open the Extrude Roll-Up window.

7. Select the depth icon, and insert a value of 30 in the depth measurement field.

8. Check the Perspective box, and choose Apply. Your work should now look like Figure 11.7.

9. Select the 3-D Rotation icon, and modify the extrusion's spatial orientation until you are pleased with the effect.

10. Select Apply.

11. Select the Light Source icon, position the light source as you want it, and increase the intensity to about 130. Your screen will appear something like that shown in Figure 11.8.

12. Select the Extrusion Coloring icon, and check the Shade box.

13. Click on the From box and select light blue. Leave the To box set to black.

14. Select Apply.

After a rather long wait, you will have an extrusion similar to, but much more attractive than, the one in Figure 11.9.

I really hope that you have been able to remain excited about CorelDRAW!, even though extrusions seem to require more time spent waiting around looking at the computer than creating.

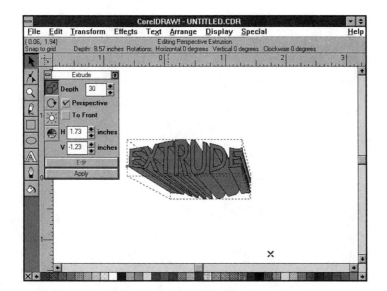

Figure 11.7

Perspective has been applied.

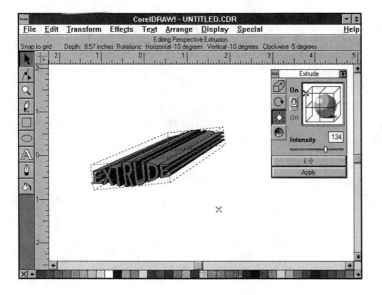

Figure 11.8

The light source has been located.

Figure 11.9

The extrusion is complete.

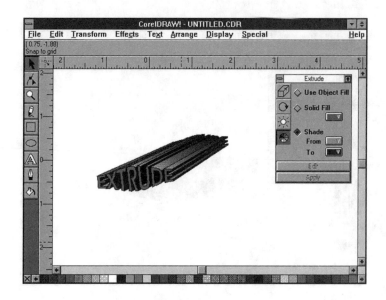

What's Next?—Blending

You can make one object blend or transform into another by using the Blend Roll-Up window. You can blend objects with different line weights, colors, shapes, and fills. Some of the effects that you can achieve are quite stunning. The following Quick Steps show how to do a simple blend.

QUICK STEPS

Blending

1. If necessary, create the first object of the blend. I used the rectangle shown in the upper left corner of Figure 11.10.

2. Create the second object of the blend. I used the apple core symbol from the food symbol group.

3. Select both objects (press ⟨⇧Shift⟩ and click on both).

The objects are surrounded by a box.

4. Press ⟨Ctrl⟩+⟨B⟩ to open the Blend Roll-Up window.

The Blend Roll-Up window opens.

5. Select 10 steps and a −45 degree rotation, and then select Apply.

Your screen should look like the one in Figure 11.10.

TIP: If your blend seems to be going the wrong way, select Reverse Order from the Arrange menu.

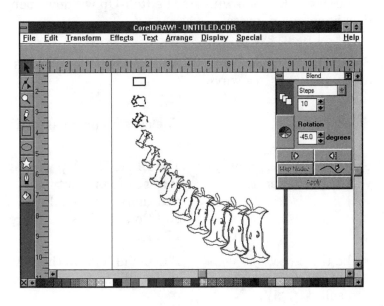

Figure 11.10
The blend has transformed the rectangle into the apple symbol in a series of 10 steps.

Blending Objects Along a Path

Besides simple blending that you just learned, you can blend two objects and have the blend follow a path. The following Quick Steps show how. Don't clear your screen from the previous example; you can use it for these steps, too.

Blending Objects Along a Path

1. Draw an ellipse similar to that shown in Figure 11.11.

2. Select the rectangle and apple that were used in the simple blend earlier.

   The objects are surrounded by a box.

3. If the Blend Roll-Up window is not open, press Ctrl+B to access it.

   The Roll-Up window opens.

4. Select the Path icon (an arrow pointing to a wavy line).

   A drop-down menu opens.

5. Select New Path.

   The cursor changes to an arrow.

6. Select the ellipse that you drew in step 1.

   The Blend Roll-Up window changes to present two additional options, Full Path and Rotate All (see Figure 11.11).

7. Make the selections shown in Figure 11.11 and select Apply.

   The blend follows the path of the ellipse.

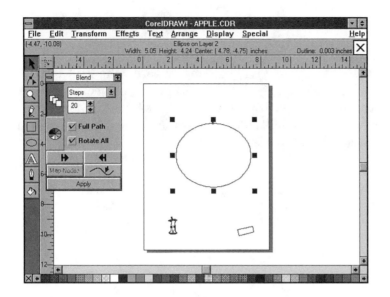

Figure 11.11
The Blend Roll-Up window selections are Steps, Full Path, and Rotate All. The ellipse is selected as the path to blend along.

When you're finished your screen will probably look something like Figure 11.12. Pretty nifty, huh?

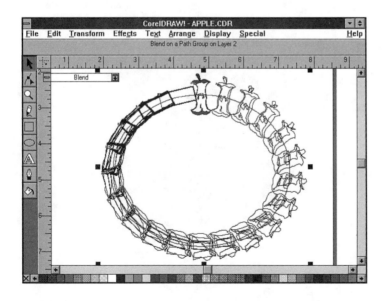

Figure 11.12
The completed blend.

NOTE: In Figure 11.1, you encountered the Full Path and Rotate All options. Full Path will put one object on each end of the selected path and evenly distribute the transformations. Rotate All will rotate the transformations to conform to the angle of the path.

In This Chapter

Color Separations

Process Colors

Spot Colors

Conventional Color Separation Process

1. Artwork is placed on process color camera.
2. The camera makes four exposures: cyan, magenta, yellow, and black.
3. The technician makes color corrections.
4. Negatives are converted into a series of dotted screens.
5. A proof is made from the four screened negatives.
6. The images are burned onto the printing plates.

Process Models for Color Separation

- CMYK model (cyan, magenta, yellow, black)
- RGB model (red, green, blue)
- HSB model (hue, saturation, brightness)
- Palette model
- Names model

A Color Primer

We are starting to see color used in every aspect of printing. Sometimes this use of color is wonderful, adding another dimension to a printed work. Sometimes, too, it is not so wonderful. No matter what your feelings on the use of color, you need to understand how those colors are transferred to paper.

This final chapter will give you a brief lesson in the history of color separations, explain the difference between the various color separation models (or *process models*) available in CorelDRAW! 3, and attempt to give you some guidance in using them for the maximum effect.

Conventional Separation Process

The conventional color separation process is still used in many publishing houses today, although it is rapidly being phased out in favor of much faster technology. The conventional process involves the following stages.

The original artwork or photo is placed on a "process color camera." This is a highly accurate camera with color-corrected lenses and an enhanced filtering ability.

The process color camera then makes four exposures: cyan, magenta, yellow, and black (CMYK for short). Each of these exposures, often called *intermediate negs* or *inter-negs*, are then examined by craftsmen who can hand-work them to the correct colors. This is the real strength of the conventional separation process. In the hands of an artist, colors can be manipulated at this stage with superb results.

The next step in the conventional process is the conversion of the negatives into a series of *screens*. This process breaks the colors in the CMYK negatives into a series of dots of varying sizes. (The lithographic process cannot reproduce solid colors; this is why you can see dots whenever you examine a printed page closely.)

A *proof* is then made from the four screened negatives (or positives). This is a close representation of how the art will appear when printed. Some modifications can still be made at this point, but one way that is guaranteed to get a publisher mad—and to drive editorial-types up the wall—is to make a practice of requesting changes this late in the game. The final step is stripping the finished negatives or positives into position, and burning the images onto the printing plates.

Although scanners are replacing the process color camera, this separation procedure is still the one used most commonly.

Color Separations in CorelDRAW!

A very good question to ask at this point is: "Why do I have to worry about color separations at all? My monitor is showing just the shade of blue I want—why mess with a good thing?"

I suppose one answer would be to wait for five or so years until the commonly-used technologies catch up with your request, because they will, without doubt. However, most printing houses still need to burn plates in one form or another, and for this they need the color *seps* (separations) to determine just what percentage of what base colors went into making that baby blue.

Making color separations within CorelDRAW! closely mimics the traditional procedure, with the exceptions that the computer acts as the process color camera, and a service bureau or high-end color printer produces the negatives.

Process Colors

Figure 12.1 shows the Uniform Fill dialog box. This box opens when you select Edit from the Fill Roll-Up window. (You will obtain the same box, with a different title, if you select Edit from the Outline Roll-Up window.)

The CMYK Model

The upper right-hand corner of the box allows you to choose between two color methods, **P**rocess or **S**pot. Select the Process method. The **Mo**del selection box should read CMYK at this point. Change it if it doesn't.

This box gives you a very good idea of how color separations on the CMYK model work. There is a white dot in the upper right-hand corner of the color box. Click on this dot and drag it into the middle of the box. You will "make" a new color that is composed of a certain percentage of cyan, magenta, yellow, and black. For example, if you take a screen that is 34% cyan, add a screen that is 25% magenta, another that is 43% yellow, and lastly one that is 25% black, you will obtain an interesting—but unnamed—shade of green. (You *could* save it and name it Zucchini Attack.)

The major advantage of using this CMYK model is that it is the one used most widely; many art-supply stores can provide you with color swatch books that are based on it.

Figure 12.1
The Uniform Fill dialog box.

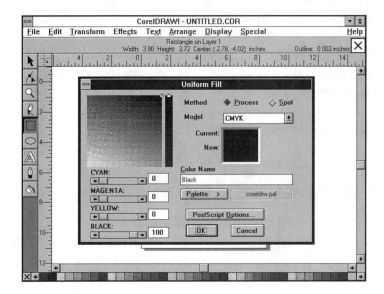

TIP: Go with the percentages, not with what you see. There is a wide variation of quality and fidelity among computer monitors and video cards. If your color swatch book tells you that red is 0% cyan, 100% magenta, 100% yellow and 0% black, and your display shows a deep burgundy when you input these percentages in the boxes, *believe the numbers.*

The RGB Model

Click on the arrow in the Model box and select RGB. The Uniform
Fill dialog box will change into that shown in Figure 12.2.

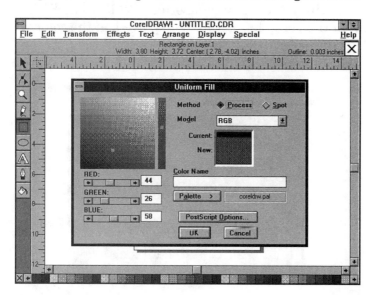

Figure 12.2
*The RGB process
model.*

This model offers you exactly the same range of colors that
you have under the CMYK model. Some people—especially old-
line computer types—find the RGB easier to work with, since this
is the way that computers tend to define color.

When colors are output under this model, they are translated
into the CMYK model by the CorelDRAW!

TIP: In all the process models, you have the option to over-
print if you are outputting to a PostScript printer or device.
You can access this option by using the PostScript Options
button; this causes the selected object to print on top of the
object beneath it. Printers sometimes call this process *trapping*. It prevents those gaps you sometimes see where one
object does not quite line up with another, and unwanted
white space is visible between the objects.

The HSB Model

If you select the HSB model, the Uniform Fill Dialog box will change into one similar to that shown in Figure 12.3. You will notice that this box differs from both the CMYK and RGB models in that all the possible colors are displayed on the color wheel.

Figure 12.3
The HSB model.

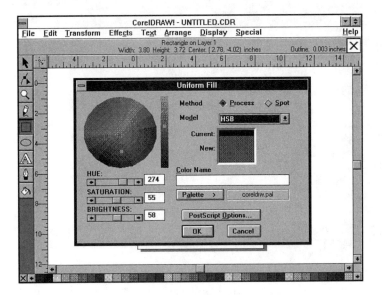

The HSB model defines colors as differing values of hue, saturation, and brightness. Click on the little square box in the circle and drag it around. You will see the color change in the box labeled New.

At the outer edge of the circle, all of the colors are fully saturated (a 100% screen can be a helpful way to think about it). As you approach the center, the level of saturation diminishes. Brightness is shown by the vertical fountain on the right side of the circle.

The HSB model is most often used by individuals with a fine arts background, as this is how color composition is often taught.

The Palette Model

Selecting Palette will change the Uniform Fill dialog box to that shown in Figure 12.4. This is a representation of all of the colors that have been predefined, and it is quite useful for projects that do not demand exacting color matches.

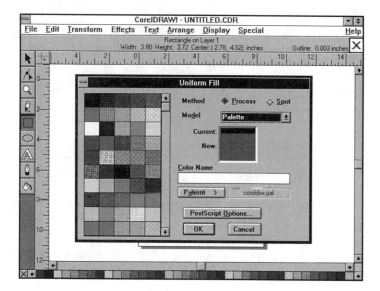

Figure 12.4
The Palette model.

This is, in actuality, simply an expanded version of the color selection bar at the bottom of the CorelDRAW! screen. When you select one of these colors and then output it, it will be translated automatically into the proper CMYK values.

The Names Model

Names—as you can see from Figure 12.5—is simply a listing of those colors that have been named. In each of the previous models, you have the ability to "invent" a new color and give it a name in the Color Name box.

Figure 12.5
The Names model.

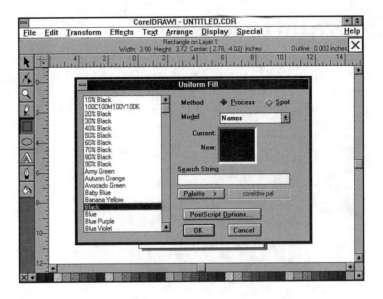

The Names model is particularly useful when using predefined colors, especially those you have invented. If you know you want to use that color you called Zucchini Attack, you can find it here, and apply it to the appropriate object in your drawing.

Spot Colors

In the minds of many print people the words "Spot Colors" and the trade name "PANTONE" are synonymous. In the world of high-end graphics, the PANTONE Palette is the language that all service bureaus, printing houses, editorial, publishing, production, and advertising personnel have in common.

When you select the Spot button, you will be greeted with the PANTONE Palette. You can select either the visual representation as shown in Figure 12.6, or you can elect to list the colors by name in the Model drop-down menu.

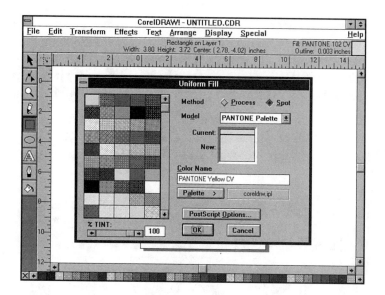

Figure 12.6
The PANTONE Palette.

You will use this palette when there can be no misunderstanding about the exact shade of color wanted. PANTONE 193 CV is exactly the same shade and intensity wherever in the world you are. You might have a PANTONE color book around somewhere. If so, you will see a whole bunch of different colors, each with a unique name.

PostScript Options

The PostScript printing options for Spot colors provide some additional ways to modify the appearance of the printed image. If you remember the introduction to this section, you will recall that a continuous-tone image needs to be translated into a series of dots if it is to be printed. A Halftone Screen is the tool that accomplishes this within CorelDRAW!.

There are three different types of halftone screens available in CorelDRAW!, and they are defined by the shape of the halftone dots. The first, called Default, uses the printer's default parameters. For a 300-DPI laser printer, these are usually in the area of a dot screen with 60 lines per inch at an angle of 45 degrees.

The halftone screen can also be composed of dots or lines of differing frequencies and angles. These are set in the Frequency and Angle selection boxes of the PostScript Options menu (see Figure 12.7).

Figure 12.7
PostScript Options
Menu

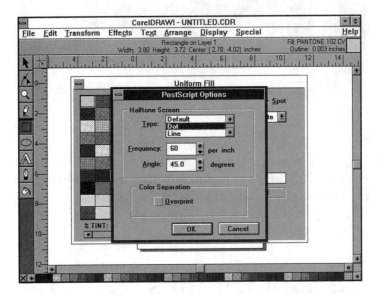

The main purpose in selecting **O**verprint Color Separation is the same as in the process colors. It is used to create a trap, avoiding those white spaces where objects don't quite meet. Spot colors can also be overprinted to create certain unusual visual effects.

Summary

As you may have guessed, a discussion of color is not for the timid. It is a highly advanced topic—one that you will always be learning something new about—and the source of many differences in opinion.

The best way to learn about color is to be very lucky and find one of those rare old-timers who has been through it all, but has had the wisdom to stay current with the state of the trade. Barring that stroke of luck, take a trip to a local service bureau and ask questions.

Well, now you've come to the end of *The First Book of CorelDRAW!*. Since this book was intended to be just that—your first book on the subject—I hope you'll continue to learn more about this complex, powerful program. The appendices that follow provide some additional information. The CorelDRAW! manual is another excellent source of information.

Using DISKCOPY to Make Backup Disks

Before you install any program on your hard disk or run it from your floppy drive, make *backup copies* of the original program disks to avoid damaging the original disks. (Although you don't have to format the blank disks before you begin, the disks must match the program disks in number, size, and density.)

Before using DISKCOPY, write-protect the original disks. For 3 ½" disks, slide the write-protect tab so you can see through the window. For 5 ¼" disks, apply a write-protect sticker over the write-protect notch.

1. Change to the drive and directory that contains the DOS DISKCOPY file. For example, if the file is in the C:\DOS directory, type `cd\dos` at the C:> prompt, and press Enter.

2. Type `diskcopy a: a:` or `diskcopy b: b:`, depending on which drive you're using to make the copies, and press Enter.

3. Insert the original program disk you want to copy into the specified drive and press Enter.

4. Follow the on-screen messages to complete the process.

5. Remove the disk from the drive, and label it to match the name of the original program disk.

6. Repeat the process until you have copies of all the program disks.

Microsoft Windows Primer

Microsoft Windows is a *graphical user interface (GUI)* which runs on top of DOS (your computer's Disk Operating System). Although many users consider the Windows screen (interface) easier to use, you need to know how to use it before it will seem easy.

With a graphical user interface, you don't type commands. Instead, you use a pointing device, usually a mouse, to select the command from a menu or to select a graphic symbol (icon) from the screen.

In addition to a graphical interface, Windows offers a *multitasking* environment. What this means is that you can run two or more programs at the same time (each in a separate window) and smoothly switch from one program to the other.

Starting Windows

To start Windows, follow these steps:

1. Change to the drive that contains your Windows files. For example, type `c:` at the DOS prompt and press Enter.
2. Change to the directory that contains your Windows files. For example, if the name of the directory is WINDOWS, type `cd\windows` at the prompt, and press Enter.
3. Type `win` and press Enter. DOS starts Windows. The Windows title screen appears for a few moments, and then you see a screen like the one in Figure B.1.

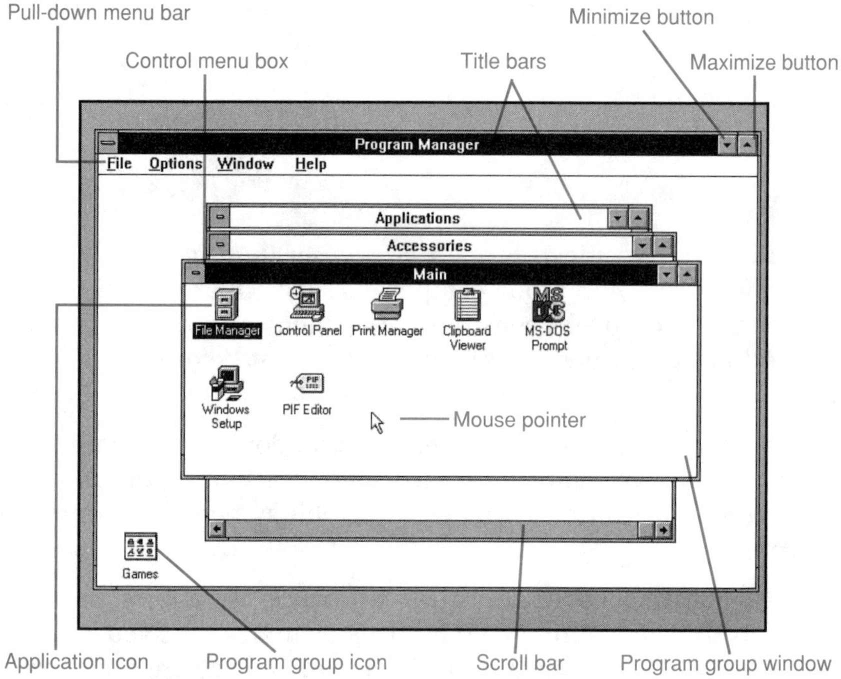
Pull-down menu bar
Minimize button
Control menu box
Title bars
Maximize button
Program Manager
File Options Window Help
Applications
Accessories
Main
File Manager
Control Panel
Print Manager
Clipboard Viewer
MS-DOS Prompt
Windows Setup
PIF Editor
Mouse pointer
Games
Application icon
Program group icon
Scroll bar
Program group window

Figure B.1
The Program Manager allows you to run other programs from Windows.

The Windows Interface

As shown in Figure B.1, the Windows interface contains several unique elements. The following list gives a brief description of each element:

- *Title bar:* The title bar at the top of the window contains the name of the window or program.

- *Program group windows and icons:* Each program group window contains application icons. You can shrink any window down to the size of an icon to clear screen space.

- *Application icons:* To run an application, you select one of these icons from a program group window.

- *Minimize and Maximize buttons:* The Minimize button shrinks the window to the size of an icon. The Maximize button expands the window to take up most of the screen. The button then changes to a double-headed *Restore* button, which allows you to return the window to its original size.

- *Control menu box:* At the upper left corner of the active window is a Control menu box. Selecting this box pulls down a menu which allows you to control the size and location of the window.

- *Pull-down menu bar:* This bar contains a list of the pull-down menus available in the program.

- *Mouse Pointer:* Somewhere on the screen, a mouse pointer should appear (if you are using a mouse). If you don't see it, move the mouse to bring the pointer into view.

- *Scroll bars:* If a window contains more information than can be displayed, a scroll bar appears. Use the scroll arrows on each end of the bar to scroll incrementally. Drag the scroll box along the bar to scroll more quickly.

Using a Mouse

To work most efficiently in Windows, you should use a mouse. You can press mouse buttons and move the mouse in various ways to change the way it acts:

Point means to move the mouse pointer onto the specified item. Part of the mouse pointer must be touching the item.

Click on an item means to move the pointer onto the specified item and press the mouse button once. Unless specified otherwise, use the left mouse button.

Double-click on an item means to move the pointer onto the specified item and press and release the mouse button twice quickly.

Drag means to move the mouse pointer onto the specified item, hold down the mouse button, and move the mouse while holding down the button.

Figure B.2 shows how to use the mouse to perform common Windows activities, including running programs and moving and resizing windows.

Figure B.2

Use your mouse to control Windows.

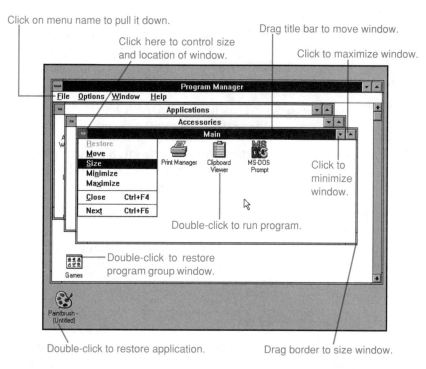

Click on menu name to pull it down.

Click here to control size and location of window.

Drag title bar to move window.

Click to maximize window.

Click to minimize window.

Double-click to run program.

Double-click to restore program group window.

Double-click to restore application.

Drag border to size window.

Using the Keyboard

Although Windows works best with a mouse, you can use your keyboard, as well. The following keyboard shortcuts explain how.

Table B.1
Keyboard shortcuts.

Press	To
Alt + Esc	Cycle through the application windows and icons.
Ctrl + F6 (or Ctrl + Tab ↹)	Cycle through program group icons and windows.
Alt + Space bar	Open the Control menu for an application window or icon.
Alt + -	Open the Control menu for a program group window or icon.
Arrow keys	Move from one icon to another in the active window.
Alt (or F10)	Activate the pull-down menu bar.
Alt + menu letter	Pull down a menu from the menu bar.
↵Enter	Run the application whose icon is highlighted, or restore a window that's been reduced to an icon.
Esc	Close a menu or dialog box.
Ctrl + Esc	View the task list, which allows you to switch to a different program.
F1	Get help.
Ctrl + F4	Minimize the selected program group window.
Alt + F4	Exit the active application or exit Windows.
Alt + Tab ↹	Switches among active applications.

Managing Directories and Files

Windows includes a special program called the File Manager, which simplifies many of the DOS file-related tasks, including listing, copying, and deleting files. To open the File Manager, double-click on the File Manager icon in the Main Program Group window. If the Main window is not shown, pull down the Window

menu and select Main. The following list tells you how to move
around in the File Manager:

- To change drives, click on the drive letter at the top of the
  Directory Tree window. Or, press the `Tab` to move up to
  the drive list, highlight a drive letter with the arrow keys,
  and press Enter.

- To display the subdirectories of a directory, click on the
  plus sign to the left of the directory's name, or highlight
  the directory and press `+`. To reverse the process, press
  the hyphen (`-`) key or click on the minus sign.

- To open a directory, double-click on it or highlight it and
  press Enter. You can open more than one directory window at a time.

- To activate a directory window, click anywhere on the
  window or use the Control menu to switch windows.

- To close the File Manager, pull down the File menu and
  select Exit or double-click on the Control menu box in the
  upper left corner of the screen.

Making Directories with the File Manager

1. Highlight the directory under which you want the new
   directory.

2. Pull down the File menu and select Create Directory.

3. Type the name of the new directory in the dialog box.

4. Click on OK or press Enter.

Selecting Files To Copy, Move, or Delete

Before you can copy, move, or delete files, you must select the files
using one of the following methods.

With the Mouse:

- To select a group of consecutive files, hold down ⇧Shift and click on the first and last files in the group.

- To select a group of nonconsecutive files, hold down Ctrl and click on each file. To deselect a file, click on it again.

With the Keyboard:

- To select a group of consecutive files, highlight the first file, hold down ⇧Shift, and use the arrow keys to stretch the highlight over the desired group.

- To select a group of nonconsecutive files, press ⇧Shift + F8, and then select each file by highlighting it and pressing the Space bar. To deselect a file, highlight it and press the Space bar.

Copying Files

1. Select the files you want to copy.

2. Pull down the File menu and select Copy, or press F8. The Copy dialog box appears.

3. Type the destination drive, directory, and file name in the To: text box.

4. Press the Copy button. Windows copies the file to the location you specified.

    You can also drag files from one File Manager drive window to another to copy them.

Moving Files

1. Activate the directory window for the directory that contains the files you want to move.

2. Select the files you want to move.

3. Pull down the File menu and select Move, or press F7.

The Move dialog box appears, prompting you to specify a destination directory for the selected files.

4. Type a complete path to the destination directory, and then press the Move button on-screen. The selected files are moved to the destination directory you specified.

You can also hold down Alt and drag files from one File Manager drive window to another to move them.

Deleting Files

1. Select the files you want to delete.

2. Pull down the File menu and select Delete. The Delete dialog box appears prompting you to confirm the operation.

3. Choose OK to delete the selected files, or Cancel to cancel the operation.

For More Information . . .

For more information about using Windows, try these other books:

10 Minute Guide to Windows 3.1

The First Book of Windows 3.1

Learning Windows 3.1

Installing CorelDRAW!

System Requirements

Corel Systems recommends the following minimum system parameters:

- A 386- or 486-based CPU. (An 80286 will perform—after a fashion—if it has sufficient memory to run in Windows Standard mode.)

- Microsoft Windows 3.1

NOTE: Even though CorelDRAW! Version 3.0 will run under Microsoft Windows 3, it is not recommended since the Object Linking and Embedding features of Windows 3.1 will not be implemented. Additionally, you must use the WINHELP.EXE file from Windows 3.1 if you wish to run CorelDRAW!'s online help.

- At least 2M of memory.

> **NOTE:** Corel recommends at least 2M of memory. I feel a more realistic amount would be 4M. In any event, you need enough additional memory to allow Windows to run in either Enhanced or Standard mode. CorelDRAW! Version 3.0 does not support Windows Real mode.

- A graphics monitor with at least VGA resolution.
- A pointing device supported by Microsoft Windows.
- A printer supported by Microsoft Windows.

Installing CorelDRAW!

> **NOTE:** Disk #1 contains a file called README.TXT. This file can be read by any editor, and it contains any information that has been discovered or added since the manuals were printed. Take a moment to read this file before proceeding with the installation procedure.

In addition to the main application, CorelDRAW! Version 3.0, the installation disks contain CorelTRACE!, CorelMOSAIC!, Corel PHOTO-PAINT, and Ccapture. If you choose to install all of the applications, filters, and fonts you will need 23M of free disk space. A full installation can take 30 minutes or more.

The applications are installed from the Windows Program Manager. To begin:

1. Start windows (type `win` at the c:\ prompt).

2. Select **R**un from the Program Manager's **F**ile menu.

3. In the Command Line field of the dialog box, type the following: `A:\SETUP`. (If you are installing from another

drive, B: for instance, substitute the appropriate letter in the setup statement. For example, `B:\SETUP`.)

4. Select OK. The screen shown in Figure C.1 will appear.

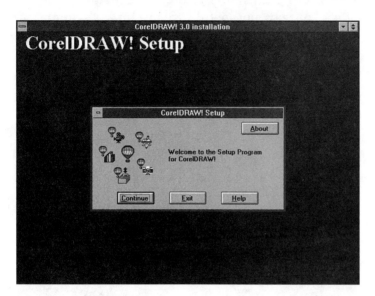

Figure C.1
The opening screen of the installation procedure.

Select Continue and, after a short time (during which CorelDRAW! scans your current system configuration), the second installation screen opens, shown in Figure C.2.

If you choose the full installation or the minimum installation, you will have no further choices to make. Carefully follow all the instructions that are presented on the screen, and CorelDRAW! will install itself.

NOTE: The **M**inimum Installation option is all that is necessary to fully benefit from this book.

On the other hand, if you select the custom installation option, the dialog box in Figure C.3 will open. Here you can select which applications to install, and even which pieces of particular applications you may want to install. This dialog box provides you with information on the size of each tool, as well as telling you how much room you may have on your hard disk.

The All and None selections are straightforward. However, if you selected the Some option for any of the tools, you would be presented with an additional dialog box like the one for the CorelDRAW! program shown in Figure C.4. Here you can choose to save disk space by not installing the clip art, samples, or even the online help.

Figure C.2
The Installation Options screen.

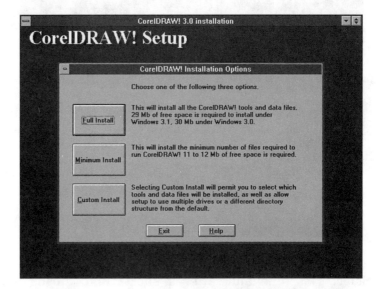

Figure C.3
CorelDRAW! custom installation dialog box.

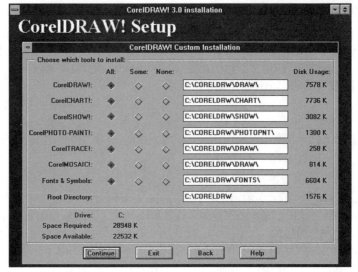

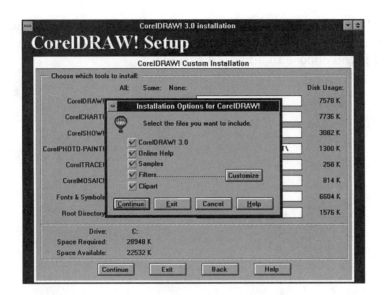

Figure C.4
Installation Options for CorelDRAW! dialog box.

If you choose, you can even further refine the installation process by selecting which filters you want to include on your hard disk. Selecting the Customize filters button will open up the Filter Selection Window shown in Figure C.5. Here you can select which filters not to install.

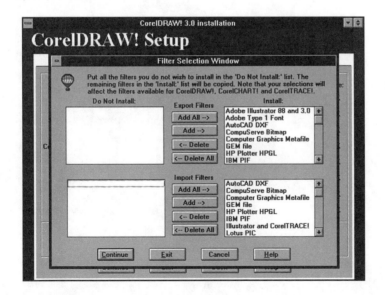

Figure C.5
The Filter Selection Window.

Carefully follow all instructions that are presented on the screen. Remember that you can run the setup program at a later date if you choose to add applications.

Customizing CorelDRAW!

CorelDRAW! can be customized in several ways. This final appendix will briefly discuss some of the ways that you can individualize your desktop.

Setting General Preferences

If you select Preferences from the Special menu, the dialog box shown in Figure D.1 will open.

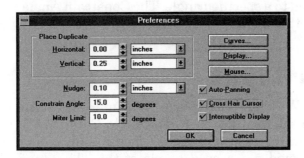

Figure D.1
The Preferences dialog box.

Place Duplicate

The Place Duplicate area sets the offset of duplicates with respect to the original object. In English, that means that when you duplicate an object, the copy will be placed at the location of these measurements—for example, one-half inch above and to the right of the original.

Positive numbers in the Horizontal field will offset the duplicate to the right of center, while negative numbers will offset the duplicate to the left of center. Positive numbers in the Vertical field will offset the duplicate above the original, while negative ones will offset it below.

If, for example, you wanted to have duplicates placed directly one inch below the original, the horizontal measurement would be zero while the vertical would be –1.00.

Nudge

Placing a measurement in the Nudge box allows you to move an object by pressing the direction keys on the keyboard. Highly accurate movements can be accomplished with this feature.

Constrain Angle

When you hold down Ctrl while skewing or rotating objects, drawing in freehand mode, or adjusting control points when drawing curves in Bézier mode, the motion of the object is constrained to a specified angle. The Constrain Angle field allows you to set this angle.

Miter Limit

CorelDRAW! joins lines much the same way that a carpenter joins boards. If two lines meet at an angle, CorelDRAW! will create a seam that runs at a diagonal. The casing around a door or window provides a good example of this. This kind of joint is called a miter joint.

Miter joints do create a problem when the angle of the two lines is very shallow: the point is very sharp and the taper of the joint is very long. CorelDRAW! allows you to select the lower limit for creating miter joints at the corners of objects by setting the Miter Limit field. Any angle more shallow (lower) than this number will be beveled (smoothed off). This avoids corner points that extend too far at very small angles.

Auto-Panning

When checked, the Auto-Panning box will cause the page to scroll automatically whenever you drag an object beyond the visible portion of the desktop.

Cross Hair Cursor

The Cross Hair Cursor box, when checked, will turn the screen cursor into a set of cross hairs that extend the length and width of the editing window.

Interruptible Display

The Interruptible Display box is quite useful when you are working with a complex drawing. When this box is checked, you can interrupt a screen redraw by clicking with the mouse or selecting any key. The redraw will suspend, and you can perform another action before it continues.

Setting Curve Preferences

When you select Curves from the Preferences dialog box, the Preferences—Curves dialog box opens, as shown in Figure D.2. The options in this dialog box are discussed in the following sections.

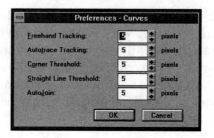

Freehand Tracking

Freehand Tracking controls how closely CorelDRAW! duplicates your movements when it is calculating Bézier curves in a freehand drawing. The higher the number, the looser the tracking. For example, a setting of 2 pixels will result in a curve that follows every dip of a drawing, while a setting of 8 pixels will smooth out the bumps considerably.

Autotrace Tracking

Autotrace Tracking controls how closely Autotrace tracks edges when it constructs Bézier curves. Low numbers result in tight tracking, while higher ones result in looser tracking.

Corner Threshold

Corner Threshold controls the point where CorelDRAW! determines what is a smooth corner and what is a cusp. Low numbers predispose CorelDRAW! towards cusps, while higher numbers will make smooth corners the preference.

Straight Line Threshold

Straight Line Threshold controls the point where CorelDRAW! determines if a segment is a straight line or a curve type. Low numbers predispose CorelDRAW! toward segments as curves, while higher numbers make the preference in favor of straight lines.

AutoJoin

The AutoJoin feature of CorelDRAW! is designed to save the artist a lot of time when drawing shapes. This feature tells the program to join any two lines whose ends are within a stipulated distance of each other.

This distance is set here. The lower the number, the closer the two ends have to be to be automatically joined. You might choose a low number if you were drawing a highly complex object and wanted to make details highly precise, or a high number if you were outlining an object.

Setting Display Preferences

Selecting the **D**isplay button in the Preferences dialog box will open the Preferences—Display dialog box, shown in Figure D.3. The following sections describe its options in detail.

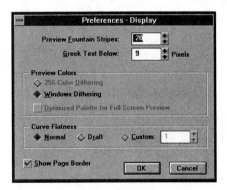

Figure D.3

The Preferences— Display dialog box.

Preview Fountain Stripes

Preview **F**ountain Stripes sets the number of stripes that are shown on the screen (and printed by nonPostScript printers). Lowering this number will improve the time it takes to redraw some files, but it can also adversely affect printing quality.

Greek Text Below

The slowest part of any drawing program is the communication between the computer and the monitor. It can take an awfully long time to paint an image on the computer screen, and often much of this time is spent drawing text.

The screen paint, or redraw, time can be shortened considerably if the computer substitutes a series of small rectangles for text of a certain size or below. These small rectangles are referred to as Greek Text. If you have a page that contains a lot of small print, you may wish to set this number at a size that will eliminate the need for the computer to draw all of it.

This option only affects the appearance of the text on the computer's monitor; it has no effect on the printed image.

Preview Colors

The Preview Colors section offers up to three options depending on the screen driver and the capabilities of your system. These options do not change the way any work is printed—only how it is displayed on the monitor.

The **W**indows Dithering mode most often provides the fastest screen redraws, but since it only utilizes the 16-color palette, your display may not be as brilliant. **W**indows Dithering will be the default if your system is set up to operate in 16-color mode.

If your system is set up to take advantage of a 256-color palette, the 256-Color **D**ithering option will be the default value. The **O**ptimized Palette for Full Screen Preview option provides the widest range of possible colors.

Curve Flatness

The Curve Flatness options provide another way to speed up screen redraws. The higher the number, the less precision is used to draw curves, and the faster the screen can redraw. The **N**ormal selection represents the highest precision, represented by the number 1, while the **Dr**aft selection represents the least precision, represented by the number 5. You can select **C**ustom to choose any value between 1 and 5.

NOTE: If you have modified any of these settings and find that your print quality on a nonPostScript printer has deteriorated, switch the display settings back to the defaults.

Customizing the Secondary Mouse Button

Selecting the **M**ouse button in the Preferences dialog box will open up the dialog box shown in Figure D.4. If you have a two- or three-button mouse, you can use this menu to customize the operation of the right mouse button. The options are:

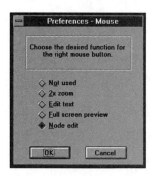

Figure D.4
The Preferences—Mouse dialog box.

Not used	No function is assigned to the button.
2x zoom	Magnifies the area in the drawing window by a factor of 2.
Edit text	The right mouse button will display the Text Editing dialog box,

provided a text string has been selected with the Pick or Shape tool.

Full screen preview   The right mouse button will toggle between a full screen preview display and the normal display mode.

Node edit   The right mouse button will activate the Shape tool.

Index

Symbols

1,2,3,4 (File menu) command, 12
256-Color Dithering option, 196
3-D Rotation icon, 150

A

adjusting
    letters on paths, 123
    path alignment, 126-129
    text orientation, 114, 124
    text spacing, 115-118
aligning objects, 66-68
alignment, adjusting path, 126-129
Apple Corps logo, creating, 120-122
application icons, 179
applying
    color to outlines, 50, 57-58
    envelopes, 130, 139-140
    fills, 90

Arrange menu, Ungroup command, 61
arrowhead selectors, 54
artistic text, 98-100
attributes, text, 114, 118-119

B

backup copies, program disks, 175-176
Bézier tool
    drawing curves, 70-75
    selecting, 70-72
Blend Roll-Up window, 156
blending, 144
    along paths, 158-160
    objects, 156-160
buttons
    Edit, 58
    Minimize and Maximize, 179
    Restore, 179

C

circles, drawing, 21-22
Clear Perspective (Effects menu) command, 134
clicking mouse, 179
clipboard, adding text, 101-103
CMYK color separation model, 162-166
color
 applying to outlines, 50, 57-58
 palette, 7
 process, 165-170
 selecting, 58
 spot, 170-172
color separation models
 CMYK, 162-166
 conventional, 162-165
 HSB, 162, 168
 Names, 162, 169-170
 Palette, 162, 169
 RGB, 162, 167
coloring extrusions, 152
commands, 8-9
 1,2,3,4 (File menu), 12
 Clear Perspective (Effects menu), 134
 Edit Wireframe (Display menu), 38
 Exit (File menu), 12
 Export... (File menu), 11
 Grid Setup (Display menu), 31
 Import... (File menu), 10
 New (File menu), 10
 Object... (File menu), 11

Open... (File menu), 10
 Page Setup (File menu), 11
 Preferences (Special menu), 191
 Print (File menu), 45
 Print Merge... (File menu), 11
 Print Setup... (File menu), 11
 Print... (File menu), 11
 Save (File menu), 42-43
 Save As... (File menu), 10
 Show Rulers (Display menu), 30
 Snap to Grid (Display menu), 66
 Text Roll-Up (Text menu), 106
 Ungroup (Arrange menu), 61
constrained lines, drawing, 21
Control menu box, 179
control points, 73
controlling thickness, 54
copying
 envelopes, 142
 perspective, 130, 136-137
 text attributes, 114, 118-119
CorelDRAW!
 customizing, 191-198
 desktop, 6-7
 installing, 186-190
 quitting, 12-13
 starting, 4-5
 system requirements, 185-186

creating
    Apple Corps logo, 120-122
    extrusions, 144-146
    shading effects, 151-152
curves
    drawing
        with Bézier tool, 70-75
        with Freehand tool,
          70-73
    shaping, 70, 78
cusp nodes, shaping, 80, 85
customizing CorelDRAW!,
  191-198

D

dashed lines, 56
deleting nodes, 86-87
Depth icon, 148
desktop, 6-7
dialog boxes
    Frame Attributes, 107
    Grid Setup, 35
    Node Edit, 82
    Outline Pen, 58
    Preferences, 191-193
        Auto-Panning box, 193
        Constrain Angle
          field, 192
        Cross Hair Cursor
          box, 193
        Curves, 193
        Display button, 195
        Interruptible Display
          box, 193
        Miter Limit field, 193
        Mouse button, 197
        Nudge box, 192

        Place Duplicate
          area, 192
        Preferences-Curves,
          193-195
        Preferences-Display,
          195-197
            Curve Flatness, 196
            Greek Text, 196
            Preview Colors, 196
            Preview Fountain
              Stripes, 195
        Print Setup, 44
        Text, 104
        Text Spacing, 114-116
DISKCOPY file, backing up
  original program disks,
  175-176
display, zooming, 32-34
Display menu, 17
    Edit Wireframe
      command, 38
    Grid Setup command, 31
    Show Rulers command, 30
    Snap to Grid command, 66
displaying rulers, 30-31
DOS, 177
dotted lines, 56
double-clicking mouse, 179
dragging mouse, 179
drawing
    circles, 21-22
    curves
        with Bézier tool, 70-75
        with Freehand tool,
          70-73
    ellipses, 21-22
    lines, 20-21
    rectangles, 21-22

squares, 21-22
    with grid, 35
drawing window, 6
drawings
    grouping, 50
    printing, 45-46
    saving, 42-43
duplicating graphics, 50,
    63-66

E

Edit button (Pen Roll-Up
    window), 58
Edit Wireframe (Display
    menu) command, 38
editing
    nodes, 82
    text, 104-106
Effects menu, Clear
    Perspective command, 134
Ellipse tool, 21
ellipses
    drawing, 21-22
    shaping, 76
envelopes, 138-142
    applying, 130, 139-140
    copying, 142
environments, multitasking,
    177
erasing parts of objects, 73
establishing vanishing
    points, 149
Exit (File menu) command,
    12
Export... (File menu)
    command, 11

Extrude Roll-Up window,
    148
Extrusion Coloring icon, 152
extrusions, 145
    coloring, 152
    creating, 144-146
    perspective, rotating, 144,
    150-151
    vanishing points, 148

F

File menu, 10
    1,2,3,4 command, 12
    Exit command, 12
    Export... command, 11
    Import... command, 10
    New command, 10
    Object... command, 11
    Open... command, 10
    Page Setup command, 11
    Print command, 45
    Print Merge... command,
    11
    Print Setup... command,
    11
    Print... command, 11
    Save As... command, 10
    Save command, 42-43
files
    DISKCOPY, making
    backup disks, 175-176
    opening, 50-51
    saving, 41-43
Fill Roll-Up window icon, 90
Fill tool, 88-92
Fit in Window icon, 33

fitting text to paths, 119-129
fonts, 97-98
formatting text, 104-106
Fountain Fill icon, 90
Frame Attributes dialog
  box, 107
frames, paragraph text,
  107-108
freehand lines, drawing, 20
Freehand tool
    drawing curves, 70-73
    selecting, 70-72
Full-Color Pattern icon, 90

G

graphical user interface
  (GUI), 177
graphics
    duplicating, 50, 63-66
    mirroring, 64
    scaling, 62
Grid Setup (Display menu)
  command, 31
Grid Setup dialog box, 35
grids, constructing, 35
grouping
    drawings, 50
    objects, 60-62
GUI, *see* graphical user
  interface
guidelines, 66-67

H

halftone screens, 172
handles, 23

help, 15
    by pointing, 18
    on selected commands, 17
    on unselected commands,
      16
    with keywords, 18-19
horizontal
    gridlines, 66
    persepctive, 134
HSB color separation model,
  162, 168

I

icons
    3-D Rotation, 150
    application, 179
    Depth, 148
    Extrusion Coloring, 152
    Fill Roll-Up window, 90
    Fit in Window, 33
    Fountain Fill, 90
    Full-Color Pattern, 90
    Light Source Direction,
      151
    None, 90
    PostScript Textures, 90
    ruler cross hairs, 31
    Two-Color Pattern, 90
    Uniform Color, 90
    vanishing point, 134
    Zoom In, 33
    Zoom Out, 33
Import... (File menu)
  command, 10
importing text, 103-104

installing CorelDRAW!,
186-190
Inter-Character spacing, 116
Inter-Line spacing, 117
Inter-Paragraph spacing, 117
Inter-Word spacing, 116
interactive mode, 117
interface, Windows, 178-179
intermediate negs, 164

J-K

kerning, 106
keyboard, opening menus, 8
keyboard shortcuts,
Windows, 180-182
keywords, 47-48
getting help with, 18-19

L

leading, 117
Light Source Direction icon,
151
line style selector, 56
lines
dashed, 56
dotted, 56
drawing, 20-21

M

Maximize button, 179
menu bars, 6-9
pull-down, 179
menu boxes, Control, 179
menus
Arrange, Ungroup
command, 61

Display, 17
Edit Wireframe
command, 38
Grid Setup command,
31
Show Rulers command,
30
Snap to Grid command,
66
Effects, Clear Perspective
command, 134
File
1,2,3,4 command, 12
Exit command, 12
Export... command, 11
Import... command, 10
New command, 10
Object... command, 11
Open... command, 10
Page Setup command,
11
Print command, 45
Print Merge... com-
mand, 11
Print Setup... command,
11
Print... command, 11
Save As... command, 10
Save command, 42-43
opening
with keyboard, 8
with mouse, 8
Special, Preferences
command, 191
Text, Text Roll-Up
command, 106
Microsoft Windows
interface, 178-179

keyboard shortcuts,
   180-182
mouse, 179-180
starting, 178
Minimize button, 179
mirroring
   graphics, 64
   text, on paths, 128
mouse, 179-180
   opening menus, 8
mouse pointer, 179
multitasking environment,
   177

N

Names color separation
   model, 162, 169-170
New (File menu) command,
   10
Node Edit dialog box, 82
node to node lines, drawing,
   20
nodes, 73, 81
   adding, 86-87
   changing, 87-88
   cusp, shaping, 80, 85
   deleting, 86-87
   editing, 82
   smooth, shaping, 80, 83
   symmetrical, shaping, 80,
      84
None icon, 90
notes, 47-48
nudging objects, 67

O

Object... (File menu)
   command, 11
objects
   aligning, 66-68
   blending, 156-160
   grouping, 60-62
   nudging, 67
   rotating, 24-25
   scaling, 23
   selecting, 22-23
   sizing, 23
   skewing, 24-25
Open... (File menu)
   command, 10
opening
   files, 50-51
   menus
      with keyboard, 8
      with mouse, 8
   Node Edit dialog box, 82
   Outline Pen Roll-Up
      window, 50
   Pen Roll-Up window, 53
   Text dialog box, 104
   Text Spacing dialog box,
      114-116
orientation, adjusting text,
   114, 124
Outline Pen dialog box, 58
Outline Pen Roll-Up window,
   opening, 50
Outline Pen tool, 52-56
outlines, applying color to,
   50, 57-58

P

Page Setup (File menu)
   command, 11
Palette color separation
   model, 162, 169
paragraph text, 98-101
   frames, 107-108
paths
   adjusting letters on, 123
   alignment, adjusting,
      126-129
   blending along, 158-160
   distance from, 125-126
   fitting text to, 119-129
   mirroring text on, 128
Pen Roll-Up window
   arrowhead selectors, 54
   Edit button, 58
   line style selector, 56
   opening, 53
   thickness selector, 54
Pencil tool, 20-21
perspective, 131
   changing with vanishing
      points, 130, 134
   copying, 130, 136-137
   horizontal, 134
   multiple-point, 135
   placing, 130-134
   vertical, 134
   rotating, 144, 150-151
Pick tool, 18-23, 61
placing
   perspective, 130-134
   symbols, 109-110

pointing mouse, 179
PostScript printing
   options, 171
PostScript Textures icon, 90
Preferences (Special menu)
   command, 191
Preferences dialog box,
   191-193
   Auto-Panning box, 193
   Constrain Angle field, 192
   Cross Hair Cursor box,
      193
   Curves, 193
   Display button, 195
   Interruptible Display
      box, 193
   Miter Limit field, 193
   Mouse button, 197
   Nudge box, 192
   Place Duplicate area, 192
Preferences-Curves dialog
   box, 193-195
   AutoJoin feature, 195
   Autotrace Tracking, 194
   Corner Threshold, 194
   Freehand Tracking, 194
   Straight Line Threshold,
      194
Print (File menu) command,
   45
Print Merge... (File menu)
   command, 11
Print Setup dialog box, 44
Print Setup... (File menu)
   command, 11

Print... (File menu)
  command, 11
Printable Page area, 7
printing, 43-44
    drawings, 45-46
    print options, changing, 44
process colors, 165-170
process models, 163
program disks, making
  backup copies, 175-176
program group windows, 179
program icons, 179
proofs, 164
pull-down menu bar, 179

Q-R

quitting CorelDRAW!, 12-13

Rectangle tool, 21
rectangles
    drawing, 21-22
    shaping, 76
Restore button, 179
RGB color separation model,
  162, 167
rotating
    objects, 24-25
    perspective extrusions,
      144, 150-151
ruler cross hairs icon, 31
rulers, 7
    displaying, 30-31
    measurements, changing,
      31
    zero points, changing, 31

S

Save (File menu) command,
  42-43
Save As... (File menu)
  command, 10
saving
    drawings, 42-43
    files, 41-43
scaling
    graphics, 62
    objects, 23
screens, 164
    halftone, 172
scroll bars, 6, 179
segments, 73
selecting
    areas, 61
    Bézier tool, 70-72
    colors, 58
    Freehand tool, 70-72
    objects, 22-23
selectors
    arrowhead, 54
    line style, 56
    thickness, 54
separations, 165
shading effects, 151-152
Shape tool
    curves, 70, 78
    ellipses, 76
    nodes
      cusp, 80, 85
      smooth, 80, 83
      symmetrical, 80, 84
    rectangles, 76

Show Rulers (Display menu)
 command, 30
Single Arc tool, 138
sizing objects, 23
skewing objects, 24-25
smooth nodes, shaping, 80,
 83
Snap to Grid (Display menu)
 command, 66
spacing text, 115-118
Special menu, Preferences
 command, 191
Spelling Checker, 111-112
spot colors, 170-172
squares, drawing, 21-22
starting
  CorelDRAW!, 4-5
  Microsoft Windows, 178
status bar, 31
Status line, 7
Straight Line tool, 138
symbols, placing, 109-110
symmetrical nodes, shaping,
 80, 84

T

testing, thickness selector,
 54
text
  adding with clipboard,
   101-103
  artistic, 98-100
  attributes, copying, 114,
   118-119
  editing, 104-106
  fitting to paths, 119-129

formatting, 104-106
importing, 103-104
mirroring on paths, 128
orientation, adjusting, 114,
 124
paragraph, 98-101
  frames, 107-108
spacing, adjusting,
 115-118
Text dialog box, 104
Text menu, Text Roll-Up
 command, 106
Text Roll-Up (Text menu)
 command, 106
Text Roll-Up window,
 106-107
Text Spacing dialog box,
 114-116
Text tool, 99
Thesaurus, 112-113
thickness selector, 54
title bar, 6, 179
toolbox, 7
tools
  Bézier
   drawing curves, 70-75
   selecting, 70-72
  Ellipse, 21
  Fill, 88-92
  Freehand
   drawing curves, 70-73
   selecting, 70-72
  Outline Pen, 52-56
  Pencil, 20-21
  Pick, 18-23, 61
  Rectangle, 21

Shape
  curves, 70, 78
  cusp nodes, 80, 85
  ellipses, 76
  rectangles, 76
  smooth nodes, 80, 83
  symmetrical nodes, 80,
    84
Single Arc, 138
Straight Line, 138
Text, 99
Two Curves, 139
Unconstrained, 139
Zoom, 32-34, 99
trapping, 167
Two Curves tool, 139
Two-Color Pattern icon, 90

U

Unconstrained tool, 139
Ungroup (Arrange menu)
  command, 61
Uniform Color icon, 90

V

vanishing points, 134
  changing perspective, 130,
    134
  establishing, 149
  extrusions, 148
vertical
  guidelines, 66
  perspective, 134
views, Wireframe, 37-38

W

windows
  Blend Roll-Up, 156
  drawing, 6
  Extrude Roll-Up, 148
  Outline Pen Roll-Up,
    opening, 50
  Pen Roll-Up
    arrowhead selectors, 54
    Edit button, 58
    line style selector, 56
    opening, 53
    thickness selector, 54
  Text Roll-Up, 106-107
Windows Dithering mode,
  196
Windows, *see* Microsoft
  Windows
Wireframe view, 37-38
WYSYIWYG, changing
  display to, 32-34

X-Z

Zoom In icon, 33
Zoom Out icon, 33
Zoom tool, 32-34, 99
zooming display, 32-34

Reader Feedback Card

Thank you for purchasing this book from SAMS FIRST BOOK series. Our intent with this series is to bring you timely, authoritative information that you can reference quickly and easily. You can help us by taking a minute to complete and return this card. We appreciate your comments and will use the information to better serve your needs.

1. Where did you purchase this book?

☐ Chain bookstore (Walden, B. Dalton)   ☐ Direct mail
☐ Independent bookstore   ☐ Book club
☐ Computer/Software store   ☐ School bookstore
☐ Other _____

2. Why did you choose this book? (Check as many as apply.)

☐ Price   ☐ Appearance of book
☐ Author's reputation   ☐ SAMS' reputation
☐ Quick and easy treatment of subject   ☐ Only book available on subject

3. How do you use this book? (Check as many as apply.)

☐ As a supplement to the product manual ☐ As a reference
☐ In place of the product manual   ☐ At home
☐ For self-instruction   ☐ At work

4. Please rate this book in the categories below. G = Good; N = Needs improvement;
   U = Category is unimportant.

☐ Price   ☐ Appearance
☐ Amount of information   ☐ Accuracy
☐ Examples   ☐ Quick Steps
☐ Inside cover reference   ☐ Second color
☐ Table of contents   ☐ Index
☐ Tips and cautions   ☐ Illustrations
☐ Length of book
☐ How can we improve this book?_____
☐ _____

5. How many computer books do you normally buy in a year?

☐ 1–5   ☐ 5–10   ☐ More than 10
☐ I rarely purchase more than one book on a subject.
☐ I may purchase a beginning and an advanced book on the same subject.
☐ I may purchase several books on particular subjects.
☐ (such as _____)

6. Have your purchased other SAMS or Hayden books in the past year? _____
If yes, how many _____

7. Would you purchase another book in the FIRST BOOK series? _____

8. What are your primary areas of interest in business software? _____

☐ Word processing (particularly _____)
☐ Spreadsheet (particularly _____)
☐ Database (particularly _____)
☐ Graphics (particularly _____)
☐ Personal finance/accounting (particularly _____)
☐ Other (please specify _____)

Other comments on this book or the SAMS' book line: _____
_____

Name _____
Company_____
Address _____
City _____ State _____ Zip_____
Daytime telephone number _____
Title of this book _____

Fold here

- -

NO POSTAGE
NECESSARY
IF MAILED
IN THE
UNITED STATES

BUSINESS REPLY MAIL
FIRST CLASS   PERMIT NO. 336   CARMEL, IN

POSTAGE WILL BE PAID BY ADDRESSEE

SAMS

11711 N. College Ave.
Suite 141
Carmel, IN 46032–9839